A Bizarre Will
and other plays

A Bizarre Will
and other plays

ROBERT PINGET

Translated by Barbara Wright

Red Dust • New York

A *Bizarre Will* and other plays by Robert Pinget translated by Barbara Wright contains the plays in the collection *Un testament bizarre* and an additional two plays: *Night* (published as *Nuit* in the collection *Paralchimie*), and *About Nothing*, which has not yet been published in France.

Un testament bizarre
copyright © 1986 Les Editions de Minuit

Nuit published in Paralchimie-Architruc-L'Hypothese, Nuit
copyright © 1973 Les Editions de Minuit

De Rien
copyright © 1988 Robert Pinget

The translations
A Bizarre Will and other plays
copyright © 1989 Barbara Wright

Published by Red Dust, Inc. New York All rights reserved

The quotations in the play *Night* are from:
CERVANTES: DON QUIXOTE translated by J.M. Cohen (Penguin Classics, 1950) pp. 934–939 copyright © J. M. Cohen. Reproduced by permission of Penguin Books Ltd.

All performing rights in this play are strictly reserved and applications for performances of this translation should be made to Margaret Ramsay Ltd., 14a Goodwin's Court, London WC2N 4LL. No performance of the play may be given unless a license has been obtained prior to rehearsal.

Library of Congress Catalog Card Number: 88-093075

ISBN 0-87376-065-4

The publication of this collection has been supported in part by a grant from the National Endowment for the Arts in Washington, D.C., a Federal Agency.

Contents

A Bizarre Will	1
Mortin Not Dead	13
Dictation	27
Sophism and Sadism	37
The Chrysanthemum	47
Crazy Notion	59
Night	65
About Nothing	75

The Stuttgart performances of these plays were translated from the French into German by Gerda Scheffel.

Other radio plays by Robert Pinget not found in this collection are: *La Manivelle*, adapted by Samuel Beckett, *The Old Tune*, first performed on B.B.C. Third Programme in 1960, published by John Calder in 1963; *Autour de Mortin* first performed on Radio Stuttgart in 1964, published by John Calder in 1967 (*About Mortin*)
Abel et Bela first performed on Radio Stuttgart in 1969, published by Red Dust in 1987 (*Abel and Bela* translated by Barbara Wright)

There is nothing that could properly speaking be called spectacle in Pinget's theatre, but rather voices seeking one another as if amazed by their volume, as if unfamiliar with the stories they are telling, so much do these stories seem to come from elsewhere.

And yet there is nothing mechanical about Pinget's characters. In the intimacy of a scene between two people, with neither decor nor objects, two individuals come together and try to make contact, to talk to each other, to express themselves.

There are many "traps": the submerged violence that may at any moment erupt during the shared "nothings" of life, a particular intonation, or breath, or pause, may tip the exchange over into the intolerable. The intolerability of living with ourselves is very much an issue in Pinget's theatre: the dialogue we hold with ourselves, which is often unthinkingly called monologue.

Traces of our history, of our desires, of our fantasies, inhabit us and come and go within us in two voices, as two "egos" fighting to the death in the hope of gaining some kind of victory, however ephemeral.

Pinget's theatre is a theatre of the voice of the human presence. Challenging the obscenity of digitalized, universalized communication, stripped of the artifices, the facilities and the hypocrisies of novelistic writing or political discourse, Pinget's plays tell us of the disorder, the conflicts and the simple joys of the living.

MADELEINE RENOUARD, Birkbeck College, London.

A Bizarre Will

A, B, *men's voices*

A. Did you see the lawyer at the time?
B. No, of course not. I was no relation of the deceased.
A. How did you come to hear the details of the will?
B. Details would be an exaggeration. But rumors, yes, and from various sources.
A. Such as?
B. For example, from one of the nephews of the deceased . . . or even from several of them. But . . .
A. But?
B. With your permission, I won't name any names. The deceased had several nephews at least two of whom are still alive but I have never seen them since. It's such an old story, all this . . .
A. And what did you discover, at the time, about the will?
B. Contradictory, bizarre things.
A. As for instance?
B. As for instance that there were supposed to have been several wills dated in different years although their wording was so obscure that it was impossible to tell . . .

A BIZARRE WILL

A. That it was impossible to tell . . . ?
B. That it was impossible to tell whether the most recently-dated document invalidated the previous ones or whether it was an addendum. Not only in so far as the personal and real estate of the deceased was concerned but also and especially with regard to a certain manuscript of which those gentlemen—I mean the nephews—each claimed to have either an original, or a copy, or a commentary, or . . .
A. Or?
B. My goodness, I don't know. All I know is that the terms of the will relating to the manuscript and what was to be done with it were much more complicated than those relating to the rest of the deceased's property.
A. What was the result of all that? What became of the manuscript? Where is it? We know there was a lawsuit, but we were not involved in that either so we lost all trace of it, although we have to find it again today for the reason you are aware of.
B. The reason, no, I don't know it. All I know is that suddenly there was renewed interest in the wishes of the deceased. He didn't make things any simpler by using different names to sign the chapters or, what should they be called, the parts, or divisions, of his document.
A. That's just it. How do you know, since you were not a close friend of the deceased, that he used pseudonyms?
B. Because of what I heard, as I've already told you.
A. But by what right? What right had you to be told these precise details—for they are precise details, wouldn't you agree?—by his nephews or by anyone else?
B. Right, right . . . ? My goodness, I knew them, some of them were my childhood friends, some were friends of friends, some . . .
A. Let there be no misunderstanding, Monsieur. We are certainly not trying to drive you into a corner and extract personal information from you in an improper manner. We are merely trying to clarify, objectively, the imbroglio concerning the different versions of the will in order to arrive at this precise point: Yes or no, was the deceased the author of these documents?
B. That doesn't come within my province.
A. But it is not a question of legal information, Monsieur. It's a question of enlightening us about the personality of the

A Bizarre Will

deceased, not in order to authenticate the different holograph wills—once again, that cannot be our purpose—but to discover whether the famous manuscript or manuscripts—we are referring to the literary work—are authentic, that's to say by the hand and the inspiration of the deceased, or not. If we have broached the question of the wills, perhaps somewhat clumsily I agree, it is precisely because of those pseudonyms that he used both for the divisions of his memoirs and for the texts relating to his last wishes . . .

B. Ah, so you know, then?

A. What?

B. That the pseudonyms . . .

A. We don't know anything; it's *you* who are leading us to suppose . . .

B. To suppose what? I'm only telling you what I know.

A. Let's not get excited. Let's forget the will or wills and talk about the memoirs. Have you an opinion about their homogeneity? According to what you were told, was there any doubt about it? Did the heirs suspect the deceased of having had some of his pages written by . . .

B. No one ever suspected him of anything at all; that word is totally unwarranted! He was the most honorable, the most upright man, the last person who should be suspected in any domain whatsoever. If he amused himself with his pseudonyms he had every right to do so, he never attributed any importance to what he wrote, he made fun of it with everyone it seems, he . . .

A. How do you know that?

B. I've already told you. I'm not going to repeat myself umpteen times.

A. Once again—let's not get excited. You may well be the one and only agent who can put us on the track we're trying to follow. The quality of the deceased's writings can indeed leave no one indifferent . . .

B. Ah, so you know his writings?

A. Forgive our inadvertence. Yes, we do know some fragments of them, quite clearly copied by different hands, but that doesn't mean that we know the original text, which is what we are looking for. We repeat that the quality of those pages justifies our interest in them.

B. I won't pick you up on what you call your inadvertence.

(*Pause.*) Hm, I'd never thought about the quality of those pages. You amaze me. You mean that even though he made a joke of it for so many years he wrote some fine things? (*Pause.*) Actually, though, I ought not to be surprised. They said he was very cultivated, unrivalled on every question of poetry, philosophy, ethics, history . . . But does culture automatically produce talent? Now *there's* a question, and one of some importance.

A. That is the question we are asking ourselves. And we should like to be able to attribute these memoirs to the deceased without having to bother any longer about his testamentary fantasies. Forgive me for coming back to them. But why did he want to throw doubt on his identity by sowing confusion both on his literary work and on his last wishes? Bizarre, isn't it?

B. Yes, that's what I said. (*Pause.*) But even so, your judgment of its quality—what do you base it on?

A. What on?

B. Yes.

A. Well . . . on . . . my goodness . . . We can't give you a lecture on literary criticism here. We are merely the spokesman for the specialists on that question, who unanimously recognize the importance of this work.

B. So it's just hearsay. You too?

A. Rumors . . . from authoritative sources.

B. So that's where *both* shoes pinch?

A. What do you mean?

B. You seem to be reproaching me for reporting things I've heard, and yet that's what you do yourselves. I should be interested to know the criteria for judging the quality of a work. Shouldn't you rather be questioning those specialists?

A. No, because as they did not know the deceased personally, those specialists, however erudite, cannot pronounce on the homogeneity of the source, in other words they can't know whether the various documents they've studied are by the same person. Plagiarism is so widespread these days . . . Not every hack possesses the necessary qualities to steep himself in an author's genius, no doubt, but some forgers, as you are not unaware, acquire such skill that they manage to confuse the issue. This has quite often happened, it's a characteristic of our technological age.

A Bizarre Will

B. So what? What can I do about it? (*Pause.*) And besides, you're evading my question, which was precise. On what criteria does one base one's appreciation of the quality of a work? And those specialists as you call them, who are they?
A. Literary critics.
B. That's not necessarily a recommendation, it would seem.
A. They are professional people who are less likely to be mistaken than the general public. Especially if they are unanimous.
B. You think so? It may have something to do with fashion, and fashion is ephemeral . . .
A. We are not thinking of contesting their authority, in this case. (*Pause.*) As for their criteria, they are based on . . . how to put it . . . a certain manner the author has of treating the subject, which implies . . . which implies . . . which implies a certain kind of mind, of disposition . . . a certain temperament which manifests itself both by its intention and its spontaneity, whether it's a question of the choice of vocabulary or of the syntax on which the tone depends, the famous tone . . . in short through the mastery of language, let's call it style, which is no other . . .
B. Than man, yes, we know. An exceedingly simplistic definition which has had its day and which doesn't satisfy us any longer. An artist's personality can be extremely diverse and manifest itself in a thousand different ways. Skill is not merely the prerogative of your forgers, it may also be that of the genius who, having expressed himself in one manner here and in another manner there, sees no reason why he shouldn't amuse himself by exploiting both these manners. Diversity, then, but a single source.
A. That's what we think too, and that's precisely why we have approached you, knowing that . . .
B. Knowing that?
A. That the deceased was not unknown to you.
B. I repeat: I didn't know him. You can't claim to know someone merely because as a child, which I was then, you've once or twice caught a glimpse of him in the company of other people.
A. Even so, that's better than never having caught a glimpse of him at all, isn't it?
B. Not much better. I tell you, I was a child. And it certainly

A BIZARRE WILL

won't answer either your question or mine. (*Pause.*) Actually, what *was* your question?

A. It comes down to this: Your judgment of the personality of the deceased?

B. I've answered that.

A. And physically—how did he look? Tall? Short? Thin? Fat? Elegant? Untidy?

B. I prefer to think you're making fun of me. What does his physique have to do with it? And in any case, I'd be hard put to answer you on that point because he had a brother who some of my friends said was very like him, although others said not. It might well have happened, in some of the circumstances I've described, that I caught sight of one or other of the brothers without asking myself which one it was, because at the time I hadn't the slightest interest in either of them.

A. Even so, you were in touch with some of the nephews, from whom you heard certain things concerning . . . let's say concerning their uncle or uncles . . .

B. That was a long time after the death of the brothers. Yes, they died within a few months of each other, six or eight I believe, and it was years later, after I'd come back to the country, that I met their nephews again and they talked to me a little.

A. And the nephews—can you tell us what sort of men they were . . . or are, since two of them are still alive?

B. There was a family resemblance. Blue eyes, and their hair . . . curly hair I think.

A. And . . . intellectually, or in their manner? Also resemblances?

B. Yes. A great independence of mind and a sense of humor which hasn't deserted them in spite of all their setbacks . . . So I was told, so I was told, because I haven't seen them since.

A. We haven't made much progress towards the solution to our question.

B. Nor have I towards mine, which is of some importance. Quality! quality! (*Pause.*) At all events, it's my opinion that we can draw a certain conclusion from the facts. If the imbroglio affects both the terms of the will or wills and the origin of the work or works of literature, it means that fundamentally, that was what the deceased wanted. He

A Bizarre Will

wanted to throw doubt on everything. Well, the least we can do is respect his intentions. And it's just too bad for posterity's certainties.

A. That is not our opinion, Monsieur. The nation's heritage . . .

B. Oh yes?! You make me laugh, with your heritage! What kind of sleight-of-hand trick entitles the nation, as you call it—which, incidentally, is a term that calls for urgent revision—to assume any rights over a work of art? What has this nation to do with the phenomenon of creation? Do you want the masses to stick their stinking noses into the most exceptional, the most individual domain that exists? The nation's heritage!—do you know what that is? At the very most it's the load of filth it's trailing in its wake.

A. That is not an opinion to be shouted from the housetops, Monsieur.

B. Why ever not? What have we to lose by speaking the truth? What do we risk?

A. Getting rapped over the knuckles . . . or elsewhere. (*Pause.*) In any case, this conversation is strictly between ourselves.

B. And what if I were to tell you that I have recorded it? Here—you see my little tape recorder? It's been working perfectly. I intend to hand the tape over to a certain radio station . . . For the innocent pleasure of hearing us talk drivel in public . . . But you needn't worry, I shan't reveal your identity. And anyway, despite your royal we, your identity is not of the slightest importance.

A. You are too kind . . . But I can repay you in your own coin. (*Pause.*) Well then . . . it's war between us?

B. War? Nothing of the kind! (*A little laugh.*) We're joking, that's all.

A. You frightened me. I thought you were angry.

B. I am never angry. Unless I'm pushed.

A. I repeat my apologies for my inadvertence which was, I admit, somewhat hypocritical. And the same goes for that ridiculous *we*, which they asked me to use in our conversation.

B. That *they* is pretty ambiguous, too.

A. Not at all, not at all. A simple association of literary enthusiasts who wish to remain anonymous. All this with a view to publication, as you will have realized. It's in order to avoid

A BIZARRE WILL

B.   leaks that we wish to proceed with the greatest possible discretion.

B.   It would be simpler, I'd have thought, and would give rise to less comment, if you were to act in your own name like everyone else, without necessarily going into your reasons.

A.   I agree with you. And now I feel quite at ease.

B.   Let's get back to the point, then.

A.   I feel a little hesitant . . . I'm afraid you'll think I'm . . . too inquisitive.

B.   Come on, be brave.

A.   Are you . . . are you quite sure that you haven't seen one of the surviving nephews again?

B.   One concession deserves another: I can tell you that I've seen them both. But I'm afraid they're in a bad state. They're only the shadow of their former selves. They only remember insignificant details, lose the thread of the conversation, keep harping on about their ill health—in short, total has-beens as they say.

A.   What sort of details?

B.   About the will, for instance; they rather think they remember that it was written in red ink. No recollection of there being more than one document, even though that was once common knowledge. They kept repeating red ink, red ink. When I asked to see the document they said that they didn't know where it was, that the lawyer was dead, that some people had been putting pressure on them, as far as I could understand, to enter into possession of the text. But what people, and when and where, it was impossible to find out. They're in their second childhood, that's all there is to it, with here and there a tiny glimmer of lucidity. Very painful.

A.   Nothing to be got from that direction, then?

B.   Less than nothing about the will. About the work—one little fact that intrigues me. They said the publisher didn't pay them a sou.

A.   The publisher? What publisher?

B.   A mystery. I tried everything to find out more, but nothing worked. I personally believe that they imagined they had been cheated after having imagined that the memoirs had been published. (*Pause.*) They said the publisher was a foreigner. That's all.

A Bizarre Will

A. A foreign publisher? And impossible to find out who? Not the slightest indication?

B. Not the slightest. I assure you that I insisted, I suggested, in short I did everything I could. Absolutely nothing.

A. Might I be allowed to question them myself? With your consent . . .

B. By all means. You'll come away with an uncomfortable idea of what may be in store for us at their age . . . Of what's staring us in the face, as they say. Me, at any rate, I'm only a few years younger than they are. Six, I think—or maybe eight? No, six. That's to say . . . Let me think, nineteen hundred and . . . (*Pause.*) Eight years younger than the older one I think, and six than the other.

A. If it won't do any good for me to see them I won't try. We shall have to go about it some other way. What can we do?

B. Those copied pages in your possession which you've had analyzed by the critics—are there many of them?

A. About a hundred.

B. And what's in them?

A. Nothing homogeneous. That's just the difficulty. There are poems, pages of a diary, the outline of a plot of a novel, random thoughts, and even some drafts of a will . . . It's all extremely well written, but in diametrically opposed styles, hence our confusion.

B. The poems, for instance—what kind are they?

A. Bucolic, I should say. Yes, there are even some translated fragments of Virgil.

B. Oh-oh! . . . And the plot for the novel?

A. That's of extreme complication. The different characters are each writing a biography of X—he has no other name—who is a dead novelist. They are endeavoring to find out, by dishonest means, how far all the others have got with their research. The surprising thing is the marginal notes to this outline. They are all in different hands, like the text itself, but they tally in the sense that they are all aimed at defining the personality of each of the . . . biographers. Even more surprising, these biographers are all described in a brief note as *nephew of* X, *nephew of* Y, *nephew of* Z . . . etc. A real headache. But also an invaluable indication, given that the deceased, our author I mean, had several nephews. We can easily liken the fictitious situation to that of the writer

9

himself, who was probably the sole author of this draft plot. He was probably amusing himself by writing in different styles, and even in different hands, and then annotating his own text in different ways too, that's to say by changing his handwriting. And this probably also applies to the other material. Incredible, isn't it?

B. What about the drafts for the will?

A. Same thing. There's not one that's anything like another. There are parodies, what else can they be called, of the seventeenth-century style, of the romantic style, and even of underworld slang!

B. Superb! (*Pause. A little laugh.*) And . . . Among all those pages, would there not be some meticulous descriptions of interiors? Country houses, other houses?

A. Monsieur! You know those pages better than I do myself! You really have mystified me! By what miracle have you . . . ?

B. I'm beginning to like you. Because you've studied those writings so carefully. I haven't read the pages you've been telling me about but I have in my possession quite a large number of exercise books whose content corresponds perfectly to the analysis you have just made. Same themes, same obsessions, same notes, same mannerisms in the writing. I've been suspecting for a long time that they are by the same hand. Your critics are right about the quality of these works but they were very wrong to hesitate to attribute their paternity to our author alone. If I haven't done what you are doing with a view to publication, it was firstly because I didn't have your pages, and then . . . how can I put it . . . All this has been bothering me for so many years that I got a little tired of it, I must admit. Unforgiveable, isn't it? I was vaguely waiting for someone to turn up and produce the missing pages by some miracle, and above all to prove knowledgeable in the matter. Well yes, Monsieur, age hasn't improved me, I'm still remiss . . . a bit of a fatalist . . . (*Pause.*) But the miracle has happened, you are here, and the exercise books in my possession are yours. Here they are. (*Sound of a drawer opening and shutting.*)

A. All that! All that!

B. All that, yes. (*Pause.*) I won't tell you how they came into my possession. That would be to reveal some secrets that I want to keep. As to the question of authenticity, I have written a little study which you see here in the guise of a preface. I don't claim that it's incontestable, but even so, even so . . . Certain indications . . . Well, you'll see, you'll see . . . (*Pause.*) Don't judge me too harshly, Monsieur. It can happen that the passion of a lifetime . . . how can I put it . . . subsides . . . It's still there, but its links with the real, I mean the palpable, the immediate, its links slacken and break . . . It's the effect of time . . . Perhaps of wisdom? This purified, free passion has thus become the ideal . . . yes yes, which we know cannot materialize but which we cherish because it comforts us . . . Our fears of betraying it have faded, it has become our inalienable possession, beyond all reach . . . (*Pause.*) Now I'm beginning to feel sorry for myself. Let's forget my ideal and think about your task. You'll have to fight to carry it through, but that's inevitable. (*Pause.*) Here—to make an end of this, why don't we go to the café over the road and have a drink to the success of your undertaking? What do you say?

A. What do I say? A drink? We'll have ten drinks! A hundred! We'll empty their cellar!

B. A great programme. Here—don't forget your bits of paper . . .

Mortin Not Dead

A, B, *men's voices*

A. Monsieur Mortin?
B. Yes.
A. Alexandre Mortin?
B. Correct.
A. Your age, please?
B. Eighty-two.
A. Is there anyone else of that name in this district?
B. Not to my knowledge.
A. Nor to ours, according to our investigations.
B. That's fine then.
A. Rather a premature conclusion, Monsieur.
B. Why isn't it fine?
A. We have no obligation nor any right to question you, no official mission, as you know. Only our professional conscience . . .
B. You don't need to apologize, seeing that I agreed.
A. Well then, it transpires from our inquiries that certain . . . how can I put it . . . circumstances . . . give us the impression that this interview is . . .

A BIZARRE WILL

B. Unexpected?
A. To say the least.
B. If you say so.
A. Then I really am talking to a man who died about twenty years ago?
B. It's amusing, isn't it?
A. For you, maybe, but just imagine our confusion . . .
B. Oh, confusion . . .
A. What are you saying?
B. It's a very widespread feeling these days.
A. Don't you attach any importance to other people's honor?
B. Whose honor?
A. That of our daily paper, *Le Fantoniard*, an honest paper, respected throughout the region, which has never been compromised in any shady business, never been subsidized in any way from any source, and which for the last thirty years . . .
B. My dear sir, you can't impress me with arguments of that nature. The press is the press, no matter what. Not that I underestimate your efforts, but you know . . .
A. You know . . . ?
B. You do your job, and I . . . do mine. Let every man stick to his lot.
A. And yours might be thought more justifiable?
B. That's not the point. And anyway, I advise you to adopt another tone and to be grateful to me, quite simply, for being here. As for your honor, don't worry, it's still intact.
A. I . . . I'm sure you're right, but I . . . I don't know how to get started on this interview.
B. I'll give you something to bite on. You believe I swindled you ten years ago, and you're now trying . . . let's say to extricate yourselves from that situation with honor.
A. It's not easy.
B. Of course it is, seeing that I agreed to let you corner me. You have all the time in the world to assassinate me once and for all, you who have so many strings to your bow.
A. Such as?
B. You've certainly thought of some, don't tell me you haven't. Big front page headline, photos, indisputable evidence, confirmation from the records office, and I don't know what . . . Scandal—a gold mine!—because you'll turn it into a scandal.

Think of your circulation, my dear fellow, you'll get your money's worth all right!
A. Then you admit that you deliberately deceived us, by . . . letting your friends talk about your death, or at least by not issuing any denial after our investigation?
B. I didn't start it. I'd been away for years, a long way away . . .
A. Meaning?
B. America, Monsieur . . . when a reliable source informed me of your intention to conduct an inquiry about my modest person.
A. And you let us go ahead?
B. I was enormously amused. You must have read novels where rich relations are referred to as American uncles? That's where they make their fortunes—in theory . . . I had one myself, although that was the last we heard of him . . . I won't insult him today by imagining that he's still alive.
A. But how do you explain the fact that your friends, your intimates, your niece, your housekeeper . . . I have the list here . . .
B. I know it as well as you do. We mustn't blame those good people. They're all dead, apart from my niece.
A. And she is that reliable source, no doubt?
B. That's none of your business.
A. How is it then that those good people, as you call them, could lie to us to such a point, and even talk about your death?
B. They weren't lying, they were in good faith, they'd heard . . . or supposed . . . or . . . Human nature is fallible . . . Imagination, fear of compromising themselves, failing memories . . . Don't forget that it was ten years after my death . . . my presumed death . . . that you embarked on that investigation, and that the people concerned were already showing signs of age . . .
A. Yes but your niece wasn't; *she* wasn't showing signs of age.
B. The dear girl! She was, and still is, her uncle's staunch ally. What a sense of humor . . . second to none! At the time I expressly asked her to play along with me—it was a game that would be neither injurious to my health nor to hers. You can imagine how we laughed about it, both in our letters and on the telephone, for weeks on end!
A. When did you come back from America?

A BIZARRE WILL

B. Six months ago.
A. But after our inquiry was published, weren't you . . . or your niece . . . risking serious trouble with the authorities?
B. What risks? And what authorities? Everyone here had either forgotten me or thought I was dead. Both the town and the county have other fish to fry than to bother about the tittle-tattle of some tabloid . . .
A. Thanks for the tabloid!
B. Oh come on, what d'you think your rag represents for the people around here? I apologize for the expression, but we really must keep things in perspective. And what do you think *I* represent—my humble self, forgotten by everyone?
A. Except by us.
B. I'm grateful to you for that, of course. But even at the time I was so far removed from that kind of vanity . . . that the chance to have a good laugh at it . . .
A. Then you admit that at the very least it was sata . . . or let's say . . .
B. Satanic, diabolical, infernal, whatever you like. I would rather say human, too human . . . You know the reference?
A. What reference?
B. Skip it.
A. I . . . Even so, Monsieur, the people we interviewed at the time, not to speak of your niece, were not all . . . gaga. Some of them were still in perfect health, as for instance . . .
B. If you mention names I shall refuse to go on with the interview.
A. Right. So you're suggesting that they had all either lost their memories, or been afraid of compromising themselves, or been so totally indifferent that they were prepared to say the first thing that came into their heads?
B. My goodness, let's not generalize . . .
A. Meaning . . . ?
B. Meaning that . . . some of them, while not being gaga—a most objectionable word—nor being afraid of the wrath of public opinion, might have had certain reasons to testify to my death . . . How can we enter into people's minds when . . .
A. Quite some reservations! What other reasons can you discern or surmise?
B. Human fallibility, once again . . . Well yes, it may have

happened . . . that I intimated to one or two of them . . . that they might get a reward if they lent themselves to my little whim . . .
A. And did they get a reward?
B. Certainly.
A. Bought? You bought them?
B. They were in need. Try to understand what that means . . .
A. We're going from Charybdis to Scylla.
B. No no, don't get carried away. Nothing could be more human or more banal.
A. You call your . . . your . . . a banality?
B. Let's call it a fantasy. And we so rarely get a chance to laugh.
A. At other people's expense—no, I can't accept that.
B. Up to you. Think about the sale of your next issue, and you'll agree with my point of view.
A. What contempt you show for our profession which is an honorable one, yes, honorable! We acted in all honesty.
B. That isn't exactly the term I would reserve for the press. But while we're on the subject, and if you will permit me a reproach, before you began your inquiries you might have got official confirmation of my death, or at the very least paid a little visit to the cemetery, it isn't very far away . . .
A. We're not in the habit . . . I mean that in our profession, witnesses are essential. Our primary concern is life, contact with the living.
B. The result . . .
A. Despite the low opinion you have of . . . the media, Monsieur, you did agree to answer us. And this business seems important to us, whatever you may think. Allow me to remind you of some of the words of the people we questioned, without mentioning their names. It won't do any harm to the ones who are now dead.
B. It's not a matter of doing them any harm, but of leaving me in peace. I've told you my age. To go through all those names, bring up my past life, avoid contradictions—that would be an effort for me, it would be extremely tiring . . .
A. We only questioned eight people, and don't worry, I promise I'll be very brief.
B. *Very* brief, please.
A. In the first place, your manservant. How long was he in your employ?

A BIZARRE WILL

B. Two or three years, if I remember rightly.
A. He spoke to us of your death in such a fashion . . .
B. He was very imaginative, very tormented . . .
A. One of the people you . . . bought, perhaps?
B. Don't let's bring that up again.
A. And your housekeeper?
B. What about my housekeeper?
A. How long did she stay?
B. Ten years, more or less.
A. She told us about the work you were engaged on during your last years. A book you were writing . . .
B. A book? Me writing a book? That's a good one!
A. But she was very insistent.
B. She must have taken my diaries and account books for literature. The poor idiot!
A. But when she was telling us about your last years, she did mention . . .
B. My death? Not much chance of that. Any more than the others, charming drunkards or crackpots. Yes indeed, Monsieur, one's acquaintances are what they are. And in any case, you certainly didn't find anyone who saw me on my deathbed with his own eyes. With good reason.
A. But they all spoke of your writing.
B. It doesn't take long for a legend to go the rounds.
A. There's no smoke without fire.
B. What a delusion! One person's simple hypothesis repeated by another becomes a third one's assertion. And you know, here too we should keep things in perspective. For you, it was a simple news item that you blew up out of all proportion. It's your job to arouse the curiosity of our good countryfolk.
A. You were . . . well, you were a native of these parts and it was perfectly normal for us to be interested in your fate. And in any case, you were less forgotten than you think, because our second inquiry . . .
B. A second inquiry? First I've heard of it. When was that?
A. Some two years ago.
B. About me? You do me too much honor!
A. Once again, we were only doing our duty. It was published under the title of *A Bizarre Will*. Did you really never hear anything about it?
B. Nothing at all. And . . . what did it reveal?

A. It was particularly concerned with your memoirs, parts of which were in the possession of one person—not to mention names—, other parts with another, and still others with . . . In short, incredible dispersion and confusion. A real imbroglio. Often it was a question of your will and its many revisions, and also of the changes in your memoirs, which it seemed you had . . .
B. My memoirs? Them again? I have never written anything in my life, I tell you. As for my will, it was made at my lawyer's forty years ago and it has never left his premises.
A. How do you explain, then, that your lawyer didn't apply for probate twenty years ago?
B. You ought to know that he can't do that unless he has seen a death certificate and been instructed by the heirs.
A. You had . . .
B. I only had my niece, who was my charming accomplice, as I've just told you. To confuse the issue she occupied and still occupies my house, as if she had inherited it. It's very simple.
A. But the lawyer . . .
B. The lawyer is bound by professional secrecy.
A. Very simple, it's true . . . But you will understand, Monsieur, after what you have told me of your whims and fantasies, why I am now reluctant to . . . to follow you . . .
B. You don't have to, if it worries you.
A. So many improbabilities . . .
B. What have they to do with the truth?
A. Would you be able to prove your long stay in America to us?
B. Here—here's my old passport, stamped by the Argentine consulate and the customs. And here's my new one, with the date of my return.
A. That does seem quite clear . . . Well then . . . where were we . . . ? Ah yes. Our second inquiry led us to believe . . . I apologize once again . . . that the will or wills were found at your house . . .
B. By whom? My niece was living there.
A. Could it have been by a criminal act, then, a burglary when she was out?
B. I repeat: My will is with my lawyer. You're very obstinate.
A. But our inquiry . . . the second one, that is . . . someone . . .
B. Who?

A BIZARRE WILL

A. Someone who wishes to remain anonymous but who knew your family well.
B. How can you believe that, I'd like to know? Anonymous! This is becoming farcical! That person was either lying or he was grossly mistaken. At all events, his statements have made no difference to my affairs; they are in order.
A. That's to say . . .
B. That's to say . . . ?
A. It so happens that your manuscripts, wrongly mentioned in the alleged holograph wills, are in the hands of a publisher who . . .
B. Be good enough not to mention those manuscripts again.
A. Monsieur, all sorts of maneuverings must have been going on during your absence . . . Our inquiry reveals that these texts do exist and, I repeat, are in the possession of a publisher. They have been subjected to rigorous expert appraisals, which conclude in favor of their authenticity.
B. Their authenticity? Authenticity in relation to what, on the basis of what document?
A. Of your letters, your papers—in short, of your handwriting. Your nephew . . .
B. My nephew? What nephew?
A. Your great-nephew, then,—or grand-nephew—acquired about a hundred manuscript pages from the person we were questioning, and they give a detailed account of your doings over many years, they describe your house in minute detail, and speak of your recollections, your worries, your aspirations . . . In short, what people call memoirs. The young man is in touch with a publishing house . . .
B. That scoundrel, that young blackguard? He'll get what's coming to him, I can tell you!
A. You mean that those . . . memoirs . . .
B. I don't mean anything at all, but I've just heard that a forgery has been committed and I'll show them, the nephew, the anonymous hack, the publisher and all the rest of them, what stuff I'm made of!
A. But your return must already have put an end to that scandalous affair.
B. No doubt. No one has breathed a word of it to me. My niece knows nothing about it, either. But I'm looking forward to

some delightful moments in the company of all those fine people. What publisher, did you say?
A. A foreigner; that's all we know.
B. I shall soon find out. And right away, to bring everything out into the open. And this time, Monsieur, *I* shall be the one asking *you* to be kind enough to grant me an interview . . . Yet I would have thought I had a right to be told without further ado who that anonymous person is.
A. A friend of your nephew's. I can't tell you any more.
B. And you say that this friend was in possession of those forgeries? How did that come about?
A. He didn't tell us. My erstwhile colleague didn't press the point, he was only too happy to observe the perfect identity of the writing of the pages in our possession and that of . . .
B. The pages in your possession? But once again—how?
A. Several sources . . .
B. All the same, it wasn't just by chance that you got hold of those forgeries. Someone on your paper had appealed to the public by . . . by . . .
A. Our literary department did put in a little paragraph inviting anyone who could give us any information to . . .
B. And the people who got in touch with you—who were they? I suppose they too were anonymous?
A. Monsieur—I really don't remember. We'd have to consult our files. All I know is that the educated public were fascinated by the whole business, and that some experts studied the different versions of the . . . well, the different versions . . .
B. Different versions by different hands? What *are* you talking about?
A. Our paper finally came to the conclusion that they were the work of a single person who must have deliberately altered the details from one version to the next, and even sometimes changed his handwriting . . .
B. A maniac?
A. A man who enjoyed misleading an imaginary public . . . But I can't go into all that again; our second inquiry covered the subject at some length. Our readers wouldn't stand for it, and I'd be in trouble . . .
B. A young journalist has to consider his reputation, yes of course. But I would very much like to know more about

this fantastic imbroglio. Perhaps you'll be so good as to tell me . . .

A. You must forgive me, Monsieur . . . You've allowed us so little time, and I still have a few questions to ask you. But you can read the interview we published. Here—this is a photocopy of it . . . You'll see what a high opinion our informant had of the literary quality of the writings . . . But I should like to come back to your niece, if you will bear with me. It seems . . . highly improbable that she knew nothing of our second inquiry which, I repeat, made quite a stir. Especially the court case . . .

B. A court case?

A. Yes. It was brought, I believe, by your great-nephew or by let's say one of his . . . acolytes, against one of the people who was in possession of the writings . . . I'm not sure which one, because I've only been on the story for a short time. Extremely unlikely that your niece would not have got wind of it either from our paper or another one . . . and even that she wouldn't have been involved, seeing that she was your sole legal heir . . .

B. There's no doubt about it, young man, you're going too far. My niece has never mentioned a court case to me; if she had, I would have reacted immediately. Your insistence . . .

A. I'm only reporting what I have been told—rather summarily, I admit. The editor sends us out on assignments with the minimum of briefing, because time is of the essence . . .

B. Well, I can assure you that there has been no court case. My honor was at stake, and my niece . . .

A. Perhaps it was to spare you unnecessary worries because she must have known—given that you were alive in America—that the only possible result of the case could be that both parties would be found guilty.

B. Once again: You ought to have gone into the matter more thoroughly. There was no court case, nor any sharp practice . . . well, fraud, if you prefer that expression.

A. You seem very positive . . .

B. Well yes, young man, positive. The press did its job—a job that I have always considered . . . well, you know what I mean. I'm not accusing you, or your erstwhile colleagues. It was nothing to do with you as individuals, you were either too young, or too enthusiastic, or too keen on fame and

promotion, which is forgiveable. It's the institution itself that I . . .
A. That you despise, yes, I . . .
B. Don't interrupt me. I see that there have been two occasions to make it look ridiculous . . .
A. What do you mean?
B. I simply mean . . . that this business seems important to you, but you ought to have gone into it more thoroughly.
A. But the editor . . .
B. How long have you been in the profession?
A. Er . . . about a year . . .
B. A beginner. You must certainly have had a chance to consult the files before you embarked on your inquiry, but you didn't—you told me so yourself.
A. But the editor . . .
The editor, however hard-pressed, would have been better advised to give you time to do some proper research. But you rely on your flair, on your gift of the gab, to maneuver an old man into a false position. Though I observe that you're the one who's losing ground.
A. You mean . . . ?
B. I mean that the first inquiry was so riddled with contradictions that any sensible man ought to have suspected that the second one, on the same subject, under different appearances . . . Well, I don't know anything about it.
A. You mean . . . ?
B. I'll put forward just one hypothesis . . . Let's say that the second inquiry, under different appearances—perhaps more logical ones—may too easily have overlooked . . . have overlooked unsolved contradictions, for example. You ought to have realized this, but you didn't. You arrive on the scene with your famous flair . . . Well, that's your problem.
A. I . . . Why more logical appearances? It's all very well for you to talk—you don't know anything about the inquiry, you didn't know . . .
B. Oh, it was only a suggestion.
A. *Did* you know?
B. My dear friend, I wasn't born yesterday.
A. *Did* you know?
B. I knew, when I saw you, that I was going to have yet another chance . . . to amuse myself. The third!

A BIZARRE WILL

A. The third? What do you mean?
B. Well . . . You admit that you have only an imperfect knowledge of this affair, and it may well be that I know more about it than you do . . . Don't look so upset, my dear fellow! You're learning your trade, and it'll have other surprises in store for you.
A. You mean . . . ?
B. I mean . . . All right, I admit that I do know about it . . . as much as can be known.
A. Then our second inquiry . . . ?
B. Your second inquiry, good God! It was so easy to get it started! . . . A simple telephone call to your editorial department, and it was off . . .
A. You mean . . . ?
B. I mean that all his life my old friend Mortier has amused himself, with my admiring approval, by composing literary pastiches whose theme was the existence of a touchy, disillusioned lord of the manor to whom we had given my name—and there you are! A very innocent game, and what a delightful pastime! And for the last time: I am no more a lord of the manor—you must have seen my house—than I am a memorialist. But Mortier has an unbridled imagination, and our converstions and correspondence on the subject have delighted me for years. Mortier lives in the town, and I supplied him with details about country life and documents on the architecture and furnishings of some of the manor houses in our region, and he wrote the admirable descriptions of them that you have read . . . As for the plot or plots outlined in those writings, the many wills, the murders, the burglaries and all the rest of the balderdash . . .
A. Burglaries, murders?
B. Yes. I must confess that they gave us some trouble, but it was so fascinating! I thought up their broad outlines during my sleepless nights and he filled them in in his own fashion. And the characters of the doctor, the guests, the members of the family . . .
A. What doctor? What characters? What guests? I think, Monsieur, that you're . . .
B. Don't interupt me . . . I may perhaps be confusing the story of your papers with other stories that are not . . . There, you see, fatigue—I did warn you . . . Where was I . . . ? Yes; I

never had any other family than my brother, who is dead, and his adopted daughter, my niece that is . . .

A. But your nephews . . . ? that great-nephew, I mean . . .

B. A stranger who claims to belong to the family, an ambitious but small-scale blackguard who says he's in touch with a publisher. Don't worry, though, we're keeping an eye on him—my niece, oh yes, as well as my friend Mortier.

A. Your friend Mortier . . . your . . . Now I'm completely at a loss . . . At the time of our first inquiry, your niece told us . . .

B. She was admirable! All that business about Africa, compromises, the unmarried mother et caetera—it was all pure invention. What a wonderful actress, you have to admit! But . . . now I'm going to refer you back to that old story, and to your files. This has already gone on longer than we agreed . . .

A. Just one more minute. After . . . after these incredible revelations, I can only suspect that you know our anonymous informant, the man in our second inquiry who gave us so many details about the authenticity of the memoirs . . .

B. But of course I know him! It was Mortier himself, he was the one who phoned you. Once again—don't look so upset! You can call us what you like, but we had such a laugh when we were preparing that interview! He's an admirable actor, too. Such subtlety, such psychological insight! It must be said that your colleague was not one of the most shrewd . . .

A. So, just like that . . . No, really . . . Carrying a . . . a joke to such a point . . . No, I don't believe you. That man was . . .

B. That man still *is*, thank God, and he's my best friend. We could arrange another meeting, if you like. Between you, my niece, Mortier and myself, no? That would certainly amuse your readers!

A. We . . . I . . . I'll think about it, Monsieur, I'll think about it . . . Yes, in fact . . . We'll talk about it again . . . The editor . . . yes, I'll think about it . . . But . . . you're really putting me through it. So much . . . fantasy . . . so much . . . I'm totally adrift . . . I'm . . .

B. Don't take it to heart, my dear fellow. You're young, I know, it may be difficult but you'll just have to make the best of the eccentricities of an old man who has nothing more to safeguard . . . apart from the odd occasion to have a laugh. He is less reprehensible than you think . . . He is ready to listen to

A BIZARRE WILL

you if you still have . . . let's say if you still have something that sticks in your craw.

A. Well, yes. There *is* still something . . . It's . . .
B. It's . . . ?
A. For the editor . . . or for me, yes, for me . . . Before the next interview—if there *is* to be one . . .
B. Yes? Go on.
A. It occurs to me that you might . . . It's a bit tricky . . . And I'm keeping you, although you . . .
B. I'm listening patiently.
A. You might perhaps tell me . . . what you expected to come out of all this . . . out of your . . . how can I put it . . . your obstinacy . . . or rather your courage . . . or . . .
B. My determination to stick to my guns? That's it, isn't it?
A. I think so, yes . . .
B. I can't explain it, my dear fellow. That's the way I'm made, and I can't do anything about it. Or rather . . . After all, old age has to be got through . . . with as little distress as possible. You'll see, every one of us, through the years, is faced with . . . trials . . . which leave us . . . both wounded . . . and frustrated. What's called life . . . It would be foolish to complain. Some people capitulate, others don't. I'm one of the resisters . . . although I don't really know why. They excuse themselves, in their good moments, by referring to great examples. I have many . . . Far too many to mention . . . and anyway, what good would it do? Everyone follows the path . . . or tries to . . . that is laid down for him . . . Laid down? No, offered . . . I . . . It's my turn to feel totally adrift . . . Fatigue, once again . . . And if I went on in this strain I'd run the risk . . . of boring you horribly, and that wouldn't be like me . . . You aren't angry with me?
A. Of course not, Monsieur. You've answered me . . . between the lines, as you might say . . . in a way . . . for which I thank you. Let's leave it at that for today, since time is short . . . May I . . . I hope to have the pleasure of seeing you again, Monsieur . . . It will be a pleasure . . .
B. A great pleasure, young man, a very great pleasure.

Dictation

M: *man's voice. Irregular delivery, hesitations, fits and starts, sudden angry outbursts.*
He is dictating impromptu to S, a stenographer.

S: *woman's voice. Very faint and monotonous.*
When M gives her the signal—by snapping his fingers—to read over what she has taken down, there is the sound of rustling papers. S has trouble in finding her place in her notes, and sometimes in deciphering them. When S says something herself, and is not just reading back her notes, her speeches begin with a capital letter.

M. Eh? What? Louder!
S. that it was more or less impossible to find out
M. That it was more or less impossible to find out or that no one would be able to find out or that no one had been able to find out but that they were looking, they were looking and would go on looking . . . or that not knowing that all their efforts were doomed to failure they were amazed that after all that searching they still couldn't find . . . or being de-

termined against all the evidence . . . or hoping against hope . . .

To find out who had broken into the above-mentioned person's house that night and, not finding what he was looking for, after having threatened, slapped, bound and gagged, emptied the drawers, knocked the furniture over, turned everything upside down . . . or else disturbed by a noise from outside or suddenly taking fright or out of hatred, vengeance, a need to hurt, a fit of rage, a former passion, frustration, premeditation, had made off with the thing he least valued, namely . . .

Sound of fingers snapping

s. to find out or that no one would be able to find out or that no one had been able to find out but that they were looking they were looking and would go on looking or that not knowing that all their efforts were doomed to failure they were amazed

m. Melodrama. Back to situation.

That was, how long ago now . . . in short, an eternity, before the time, the time we're concerned with, namely the here and now, this . . . present, this unchanged, unchangeable, indisputable, indiscernible, interminable present . . . What people call a situation.

Calm, reflexion, work, little everyday pleasures. Happiness, sort of . . . well . . . in short, inside it up to here, nauseating, what they call . . .

He has a small private income, enjoys pottering about, old friendships, old questions, old answers, we aren't taken in, we're in no hurry, certainly not, we're here, we can wait, we're easy-going.

He has a nice clean little house, flowered wallpaper, balcony with geraniums, facing south-west. The ideal. A little garden, too, or a quiet little square or crossroads. It had been fine all day, our man had gone for a walk, he'd met some old acquaintances, old questions et caetera when all of a sudden the other man comes out with by the way what about your nephew? He doesn't answer immediately, scenting inquisitiveness. And then he replies quite coolly I saw him last week, a charming boy, good manners, hard-working and everything, we lunched together, he left around four . . .

Dictation

Inquisitiveness or guile, the acquaintance was simply waiting for him to open up, to reveal something outrageous, goodness knows what, with all the gory details, owing to a providential feeling of boredom which would have made him just like that at a stroke I repeat spill his guts as they say in the gutter but that was to show an imperfect knowledge of our man who bowed and went on his way. Or to go back over these things from a different point of view namely that of an impartial observer but where's the interest in observing this boring, friendless old fogey, there's nothing there to arouse . . . Unless there's a precise reference to some peculiar obsession, not easy to see for the moment . . .

Providential feeling of boredom which would have made him . . .

Sound of fingers snapping

s. which would have made him just like that at a stroke I repeat spill his guts as they say in the gutter but that was to show an imperfect knowledge of our man who bowed and went on his way or to go back over these things from a different point of view namely that of an impartial observer

m. Namely that of a third party who was not in the least observant but who it seems was there no one knows how, and who apparently saw but where from, what through and when, dead of night, the visitor in question going in, the visitor, the intruder, the individual . . .

It will be remembered that the house . . .

Sound of fingers snapping

s. nice clean little house flowered wallpaper balcony with geraniums facing south-west the ideal a little garden too or a quiet little

m. It will be remembered that the lodging . . . gives on to a gloomy courtyard, gloomy not to use a worse word, and that a . . . and that there is nobody that might be called a concierge, a caretaker, a porter, a night watchman, a janitor, a security officer in charge of the building, three floors no modern conveniences, water on the landing, WC ditto, insolvent tenants, quarrelling couples, shouts and screams, smells, litter and I'll skip the rest, in short, camping out in all its horror.

A BIZARRE WILL

Mention a skylight in the roof? A student, a maid or someone of that sort seems to have been there and at that very moment to have climbed up on to a stool, a table, a chair, a soap box and looked out on the off chance to inspect the bottom of the courtyard but what with? A powerful searchlight?

Forget about the point of view, there isn't one. Which implies a relation of the purely . . . imaginary facts . . . so as to end up . . . so as to end up . . .

Conclusion!

Sound of fingers snapping

s. Conclusion?
m. What we posited at the outset . . . or the premises if you prefer.
s. Premises?
m. The major, the minor—the premises, all that old stuff! We've got ourselves into a syllogism!
   What's a syllogism?
   Read the premises again.
s. I . . . I'm not sure I . . .
m. The beginning!
s. that it was more or less impossible to find out
m. Before that, before that!
s. Before?
m. After!
s. or that no one would be able to find out or that no one had been able to find out
m. After!
s. to find out who had broken into the above-mentioned person's house that night
m. The end, the end of that.
s. fit of rage a former passion frustration premeditation had made off with the thing he least valued namely
m. Had made off with the thing he least valued, namely . . . life. That's the conclusion.
   In order to end up with the conclusion . . . posited before the premises . . . posited before the premises . . . Petitio principii? That old stuff! Reasoning about death petitio principii? Taking for granted what is to be proved? (*to* S): Is that it? Is that it?

Dictation

s. I . . . I'm not sure I . . .
m. Death, petitio principii!
   In short, situation.
   Exposition.
   An old fogey in a crummy lodging. Lives alone with his cat.
   Discomfort. Stench. Retired? A nest egg under his mattress.
   The fellow hardly ever goes out, doesn't know anyone, is suspicious of everyone. Locks everywhere. On the drawers, on the chest, on the wardrobe. Eats rice, potatoes. Shits rarely, pisses with difficulty. Reads old almanacs, plays patience, goes to bed, can't sleep, gets up, drinks his coffee and waits for the evening.
   The cat goes through the local dustbins.
   The old crackpot has a nephew who comes to see him every month. The old man doesn't trust him and complains that he's dying of hunger. The nephew knows the score and doesn't react. The old man asks him one day why do you come to see me? The nephew answers . . . in remembrance. In remembrance of what? In remembrance of mother. Leave your mother where she is and me with her. Oh come, Uncle, feelings. Feelings? The old man bites his tongue, doesn't finish. The nephew pretends to be sorry for him. It doesn't work. He leaves his uncle.
   Until the day when, having acquired sufficient knowledge of the premises, he decides to rob his uncle.
   So we say the nephew. Without knowing it. Impossible to find out . . .

Sound of fingers snapping

s. or that no one would be able to find out or that no one had been able to find out but that they were looking they were looking and would go on looking or that not knowing that all their efforts were doomed to failure they were amazed that after all that searching they still couldn't find or being determined against all the evidence or hoping against hope
m. A convenient hypothesis. Supposition? Probability? Evidence? That isn't the point. As the tale unfolds—suggestions. You suggest, as the tale unfolds, you search, you become determined, not knowing or not wanting to know—that's not

A BIZARRE WILL

the point—that all their efforts were doomed to failure. You're no longer amazed—seeing that you can't find out—at making suggestions against all the evidence either, since it's no longer either a question of knowing or of expecting to know but of pleasing, really pleasing, tending to substitute one gap for another, one void for another void.

Of really pleasing? Doubt about the terms.

This void then on the said night leaves his house and goes to his uncle's. Total darkness in the street, ditto in the staircase of his uncle's block. Not a sound anywhere. He starts to climb the stairs. Like a thief in the night.

He arrives at the third floor . . .

Or then or then . . .

The nest egg. Careful. They say . . . they said . . . Who's *they*? Variations on a false plural that's probably no more than . . . probably no more than a scattered singular, scattered, dispersed, disseminated, dissected, disjointed, dissolved, distorted, discontinuous . . . A convenient hypothesis, I repeat . . . they repeat . . . claimed that the old crackpot was concealing a nest egg in his hovel, you can't keep anything secret, that's only natural, and with a bit of imagination, stashed under his mattress, the sort of inspiration that materializes nine times out of ten or ninety-nine times out of a hundred . . . materializes, material, moneybags, money, mattress . . . Or that one day when the nephew was there the cat was burrowing under the bedclothes and the old boy . . . or that the nephew offered to make his bed for him and the uncle couldn't conceal his sudden agitation . . . or any other banal supposition confirming in the nephew's mind the supposition of the presence of the nest egg in that place.

The cat . . .

Sound of fingers snapping

S. the cat goes through the local dustbins

M. That's only natural. In short, that evening, our man had eaten his apology for a meal and made sure as he did every evening that his gold was still in its place and then sat down to his game of patience. Not a sound. The candle is flickering in the permanent draught. His old fingers move over the outspread cards. Desolation, degradation, derision . . .

Dictation

When he suddenly hears a faint sound in the corridor. He stands up, goes over to the door, sticks his ear to it. Listens. Nothing, now. Anxious, he waits, doesn't move. Then he reassures himself, deciding it must be the cat coming back from the dustbins . . . Opens the door a crack, calls Puss, Puss. Nothing. Reasures himself, deciding it must be the wind. Sits down to his patience again.

The other man for his part, the nephew, that . . . void, that . . . on the said night . . . This void . . .

Sound of fingers snapping

S. this void then on the said night leaves his house and goes to his uncle's total darkness in the street ditto in the staircase of his uncle's block not a sound anywhere he starts to climb the stairs like a thief in the night he arrives at the third floor or then or then

M. Stops on the landing, not sure whether to start down the corridor, his foot brushes against a cardboard box full of rubbish, slight sound of something falling . . . Actions carried on simultaneously, the inevitable is about to happen. Collision. Reader avid for sensation . . . shivers. We leave him in suspense.

Who's *we*?

Sound of fingers snapping

S. variations on a false plural that's probably no more than probably no more than a scattered singular scattered dispersed disseminated dissected disjointed dissolved distorted discontinuous a convenient hypothesis I repeat they repeat

M. An old fogey . . .

Sound of fingers snapping

S. an old fogey in a crummy lodging lives alone with his cat discomfort stench retired a nest egg under his mattress the fellow hardly ever goes out doesn't know anyone is suspicious of everyone locks everywhere on the drawers on the chest on the wardrobe eats rice potatoes shits rarely pisses with difficulty reads old almanacs

M. All old men are robbable. He's an old man. He's robbable. All nephews . . . (*to* S.): What do you say?

S. I . . . I'm not sure . . .

A BIZARRE WILL

M. If you had to complete it, what would you say? . . . (*Pause.*) The syllogism.

That was, how long ago now . . . in short, an eternity, before the time, the time we're concerned with, namely the here and now, this . . . present, this unchanged, unchangeable, indisputable present, with us inside it . . . This narration . . . relation . . . this . . . has become embodied here, we are inside it, constrained, stuck, involved, having merely intended to pass the time, the other kind of time, its vague double, vague, vacillating, volatile, evanescent . . . that's what this drama is, as hard as my head, this paper, this conventional sign . . . Inevitable.

Tear up this paper? We know.

Break this head? Ditto.

You search, you search, you find that door with on the one side the one, on the other the other. The drama in question.

Or that it's being played out somewhere else . . . in this head . . . somewhere else . . . the machine that traps signs has developed a fault, the signs escape it and go off somewhere else to become snatches of speech . . . which the machine again tries to trap in the toils of memory, an unstoppable mechanism, leading to the abolition of the movement that it triggers . . . the initiator is left stranded, far behind, he no longer has the strength to ask himself what urged him . . . to initiate the process . . . fascination with the blank . . . paper . . .

Or that the story of the nephew deteriorates, breaks off, suddenly cut off, cut short, without warning, basta, it falls on deaf ears . . . and that by chance, here or there, by the side of a road . . . by the side of the water . . . the eternal shipwrecked victim of stories . . . the person who tells them, who is the only one telling them, the sole survivor . . . they listen to him, they used to listen to him . . . they don't listen any longer . . . disturbing, undesirable . . . and the story repeats itself, it makes a fortune, and then deteriorates, falls on deaf ears, and the deaf one day by chance find the shipwrecked man on the same shore, he's the sole survivor . . . of a different story . . . the same . . . same mechanism, same listening process, same abandon . . .

So that you wonder, you search, you don't find . . . why, when, how it is that distaste, then retaste, then redistaste

Dictation

... what mystery, what recipe, what pepper, what spice ... would make this ... sempiternal ... story ... take possession of memory and never let go of it ... in the paradise of endless repetitions ... endless repetitions ... far away from sound, words, movement ...

s. What?
m. From sound, words, movement.
s. Wordless repetitions?
m. Who said anything about wordless repetitions?
s. so that you wonder you search you don't find why when how it is that distaste then retaste then redistaste what mystery what recipe what pepper what spice would make this sempiternal story take possession of memory and never let go of it in the paradise of endless repetitions endless repetitions far away from sound words movement
m. Strange.
   Machine that traps signs.

Sound of fingers snapping

s. this head somewhere else the machine that traps signs has developed a fault the signs escape it and go off somewhere else to become snatches of speech which the machine again tries to trap in the toils of memory an unstoppable mechanism leading to the abolition of the movement that it triggers
m. Somewhere else, somewhere else to produce speech but from this head they have taken flight, the words have taken flight, silence reigns in it ... or that what reigns in it, afterwards, beyond, a new head, far away from sound, endless repetitions that are no longer words but silence ... yes ... or repeats ... what reigns in it is a length of perpetual silence ... that voice finally silenced ... repeating that the voice is no longer of any use ... without words ... an absent voice ... a hollow ... the reverse of meaning ... music of nothing ...
s. Might as well stay in bed.
m. What?
s. I said might as well stay in bed.
m. Apropos of?
s. Of the music of nothing, of the reverse of meaning, of the repeat of silence and all the rest of it.

Sound of a chair suddenly being pushed back.

A BIZARRE WILL

Then of receding footsteps.

M. Mademoiselle! Don't go off like that!
S. I'm not paid for the music of nothing, Monsieur. I'm an honest stenographer. When you have some proper work to give me, we'll see.

A door slams.

M. Vile creature! Who does she think she is? Since when have stenographers . . . (*Pause.*) Actually, though, she may have some excuse. (*Pause.*) She may have some excuse . . . (*Decrescendo repetitions for a few seconds, like a cracked record.*) She may have some excuse . . . she may have some excuse . . . she may have some excuse . . .

Sophism and Sadism

Man's voice. "Theatrical" tone.

This'll be for rehearsal. Are you listening?

Pause.

He enters. He tells the story of three subjects who might perhaps be only one . . . given the intimacy of their relationships . . . namely an invalid, his confidant, and the person who listens to them and transmits their remarks. They are respectively enumerated: number one, the confidant; number two, the invalid, and number three, the reporter.

A short preliminary meeting. Number three speaks first.

Pause.

Saying . . . saying that the extreme attention he had paid him had in no way touched the other who had gone off just like that, plunged in his dark thoughts, profoundly isolated from the world or let's say from the context, a most distressing phenomenon, there's nothing to be done about it, the unhappy man becomes gloomier all the time, dragged down into the gulf by the invisible dog, the cantankerous chimera that his formerly fascinating imagination has become; yes, it's true, his imaginative faculties are deteriorating, his mind seems to have become contaminated, isn't it alarming that no cure for this disease has yet been found, if I were a medical man, he said, I would employ all my skill in treating melancholics and finally overcoming the blues . . . the blues . . .

Saying which, he too went off plunged in his dark thoughts, affected by the same disease that he so strongly deplored, lucid, courageous when necessary, but incapable of fighting alone against the ailment in question.

As for the first man, the one who had paid such great attention to the invalid's remarks, it seems that nothing is yet known about his state of health, but that it's quite probable . . .

In short, all this is grey, nebulous, has no horizon; in the last analysis it's circular, involuted and regressive. Not a very attractive domain to enter, but what can you do, what can you do?

Pause.

And that he had taken it into his head—*he*, that's still the first man, the attentive one—he had taken it into his head to write about it, or more precisely to give an account of those days spent in talking about nothing, in complaining, in repeating oneself, contradicting oneself, quibbling, equivocating, cavilling, only to go away and find oneself alone with one's dark thoughts until the following day when one would once again seek an ear without the slightest intention or desire to get either advice or support in return.

Wouldn't that go some way towards proving the justification of our suspicions about his state of health?

Because, he said, he could see no solution to the problem posed by that state of affairs other than perpetual reiteration, a sort of homeopathic cure, treating the disease by the disease, the written word being so it seems less aleatory than the spoken word, an effort of concentration, a more complete immersion in the fog bath, a tension conducive to regurgitation, et caetera. The hoped-for proof would thus be brought about . . .

He went off, then, the man who was reporting these remarks, dragged down into the same gulf, still by the same nocturnal dog that martyrized the others, which would mean that he was perpetually coming and going, a shuttle between the particular

Sophism and Sadism

mouth that he had definitely made his own, since he was similarly affected, and a particular ear.

Pause.

As for the second man, who had gone off just like that, so far as the understanding of the text is concerned there would apparently be no reason for him to return but we bet he *will*, for the same reason as the third man, namely to be listened to at all costs, to be the object of extreme attention without however expecting the slightest comfort from anyone . . . The slightest comfort.

Which implies that the first man, the attentive one, would finally write nothing but what the third one had said, and that we might therefore doubt the reality of his effort and its effect, namely the account of the pitiable fate of the second man and also of his own, for this account would be no more likely than the grievances of the others to elicit the slightest reaction from anyone . . .

Re-Ac-Shun from A-Ny-One.

Pause.

The problem thus posed, the attentive man would plunge into the difficulty of discovering why things had presented themselves in this fashion as if they were the consequence of a necessity which had not even been glimpsed during time immemorial but which had been revealed to him in a bright interval among the mass of his nebulous worries just as a high peak appears and transpierces the clouds in the evening, and suddenly turns a triumphal, terrifying red.

Pause.

For the fact of having taken it into his head to set down in writing the impression made on him by the bitter remarks confided to him, instead of prolonging the said bright interval up to a kind of mental well-being due to the bursting of the metaphorical abscess that had been growing in his brain, this fact, then, had on the contrary increased his torment and reopened the question of his situation more painfully than ever.

Now what he had to do, so as not to confess himself definitively beaten, was once again to sweep away the torrent of black ink with which the octopus of anguish had just inundated his spirits . . .

A curious or even inexplicable thing, given the touchy, obstinate nature of the subject, was that this alert didn't necessarily seem to halt forthwith all effort towards a little reflexion, privately this surprised him, but there was still some scope, he thought, for him to pursue his research into causes and effects. No doubt the aleatory element in question had arisen at a propitious moment and the bright interval had merely been the premonitory sign of an event that had long been in preparation and was independent of any act of will, an irreducible manifestation of the unconscious which was progressing by leaps and bounds towards a certain fulfilment . . .

Was it necessary . . . Are you listening?

Pause.

Was it necessary even so to go no further than the analysis of the personal case of the first man? was it possible to do so objectively? would there be many occasions for error, seeing that it was a question of himself . . . the one we have called the attentive one, in other words the conscious?

It would be wiser to concentrate on the case of the third one . . . who would be the first to report these remarks . . . or on the case of the second one who went off just like that . . .

We would be inclined to opt for the latter, seeing that he was the first to orient the present considerations towards the fathomless distress of this fatigued trio . . .

Fatigued trio . . .

Pause.

He would seem to differ slightly from his congeners in that his presence . . . in that his rather less weighty presence would have done no more than originate the text, even though we have already foreseen that he would return to lament his ills.

A bachelor in all probability, not that a married man might not be subject to melancholy but there would seem to be an almost compelling image of a man of a solitary temperament, and the case of a deceived husband is also less conducive to an exhaustive analysis of solitude.

Going off just like that, we would see him in his filthy raincoat, a bag slung over his shoulder, disappearing in the

Sophism and Sadism

direction of the marshes where he now and then traps moorhens to nourish his sick mother who is groaning on a straw mattress in a charcoal-burner's hut.

Pause.

Smoke-filled image of that windowless room, blue flames rising from the cow-dung burning in the hearth, the son collects it in the neighborhood.

The unfortunate bedridden woman cannot at first be perceived against the far wall, the door is left open to allow the smoke to clear away . . .

Then the eye becomes accustomed to the gloom and sees the mother, she is suffering from an incurable disease that has more than half-disfigured her. Her face is bleeding, suppurating, oozing and putrefying in many places, leaving only her nose-holes intact . . .

Her nose-holes . . .

Pause.

The unhappy woman's limbs are deformed and immobilized by rheumatic fever, she can no longer move either her arms or her legs. She is huddled up on her pallet and never stops weeping and repeating oh la la, oh la la . . .

Who would not be moved by this sight? Who would not be moved?

Pause.

To have to face the sight. Courage.

Arrival of the son. He puts his bag down on the table, lights a candle and says God it stinks in here. His mother gives him a humble look and murmurs—because she can still speak—my darling, I understand, if you can't bear it move me into the shed, that'll be quite big enough for me . . .

Pause.

For in fact a kind of lean-to or former rabbit-hutch abutted the outer wall of the hut but the martyr couldn't have lived in it, the cold would have killed her.

And anyway her son was certainly not thinking of anything of the sort, he adored his mother but they had become so used to destitution and lack of privacy that he no longer used kid-glove methods to say what he thought in front of the sick woman . . . She on the other hand had never lost either her refined ways—she was the daughter and grand-daughter of industrialists—or her tender maternal feelings with the result that she constantly effaced herself and sacrificed her every comfort to her child . . . which, to come back to the attitude of the son, might have caused an uninformed third party to think that such was not the case, hence that he did not adore her, because he never stopped rebuffing her, insulting her, scoffing at her, reviling her, spitting in her face, when he wasn't deliberately breaking wind noisily as he passed by her.

Pause.

These paradoxical effects of love are frequent.

Pause.

The son didn't answer, but pulled a scrawny moorhen out of his bag and began to pluck it, sending the feathers flying all over the place and blaspheming, with the intention of making his mother suffer, for she retained her very vivid faith and was still shocked by the slightest little thing.

Hoping not to provoke a new outburst of blasphemies the bedridden woman kept quiet and raised her eyes to heaven, you could see that she was praying for her child even though there was no movement of her non-existent lips to prove it.

Pause.

There's one more thing that might be said—about the entrance of the son and his remark on how the place stank—that this scene was repeated daily in the same words, first his and then those of his mother, so that when the mother said my darling I understand, move me into the shed, she knew that her son would do no such thing . . . which proves how far . . . how far not only the attitude one adopts but also the words one utters in such situations are as you might say automatic and do not express one's feelings which, far from provoking the words are remote from them, having taken refuge in the innermost recesses of the heart and only manifesting themselves on fortuitous occasions that have nothing in common with the humdrum routine of everyday life, the feelings in this case being those of his adoration of her and vice-versa.

Sophism and Sadism

Pause.

And what does the son do after he has plucked his hen? He says . . . how is it possible to be as beggarly as us, it's all because Madame used to spend money like water in the days of her glory, my poor father, how he used to suffer when he had to keep saying we must economize, oh no though, Madame disregarded everything but her expensive tastes and the moment she became a widow Madame ran through all the capital and threw her son out on to the street and Madame takes her ease in bed while I sweat and slave to get something for Madame to eat . . .

Pause.

Same remark with regard to the everyday recurrence of this fact, same remark with regard to the resigned silence of the unhappy woman and to her eyes uplifted to heaven to intercede for her loved one.

And why do you always have to raise your eyes to heaven, he adds, go on, say it, that I exasperate you, and so saying he flung his plundered game bird in her bleeding face shouting eat it, eat it, and much good may it do you before you shut your great gob for good and go and take your ease up there . . .

From which we might infer that the insulter was not unaware of the relations his mother maintained with the Creator and that it was in bad faith that he claimed that she raised her eyes to heaven in exasperation.

The paradoxical effect of love once again.

Pause.

What does the insulter do next? He goes and takes the fowl back, tears off a wing and stuffs it in his poor mama's mouth. She begins to munch the raw flesh with all the more difficulty in that she has only two or three stumps of teeth left, she can't make use of her paralyzed hands and she nearly chokes several times while her son for his part gnaws at the carcass and gobbles up his meager provender, he's famished.

There is nothing surprising about the fact that he doesn't take the trouble to cook the bird first given the absence on these premises of any kind of grill, frying pan, saucepan . . .

Grill frying pan saucepan . . .

And then he curls up by the hearth and falls asleep to the last glimmers of the cow-dung.

A sad ending to the day for this outcast.

Pause.

As for the mother, if she hasn't spat it all out or vomited she digests it with difficulty, sucking her bone, and she waits, resigned and in pain, because it is a long time since she has been able to sleep, for the dawn to show grey through the chinks in the door.

Pause.

When her son wakes up, an event that is manifested by a new breaking of wind, she recites a Pater and an Ave with all the more difficulty in that her lips, as we have seen, have left her . . . which incidentally causes the question of pronunciation to be posed. How does she go about articulating? How does she go about it?

Pause.

Are you listening?

Pause.

It is probable that her words are altered by this lack and that what little she says must be guessed at rather than understood, whether it be my darling and all the rest of it or the prayer at dawn . . .

Now her torturer is up. He lets out a mother of God shitting bastards and goes out to urinate, deliberately leaving the door open so the glacial air comes rushing in through it and makes the unfortunate woman cough frightfully.

A sad beginning to the day for her, she wonders how many more times she will have to endure these frightful mornings, these ghastly afternoons, these funereal vigils, and on top of it all she suffers for her son, which makes her days doubly interminable and doubly sad.

Pause.

Let us imagine what the weeks will look like if she is strong enough to envisage them. And the *months* . . . But it is unlikely that her state will allow of such additional lucidity, and we shouldn't pity her on that account . . .

The son comes back doing up his buttons or even not doing up his buttons, grabs the broken pitcher from the table and drinks the last drop from it with a nasty laugh aimed at his mother and this occurs every day, which implies that what water the pitcher is still capable of holding must be replaced. He does this by going outside and scooping some up from a stagnant puddle, leaving the door wide open once more, the victim again coughs fit to bust her guts or what little she has left.

Pause.

Does this mean to say that she . . . the mother, that is . . . never drinks a single drop of liquid, which would immediately lead to her decease? No, because in order to make her sufferings last, every other day the son empties the pitcher over her face and the parched woman laps up what she can . . . Which means that on alternate days the moment her thirst is quenched she feebly murmurs pipi, as if to invite her son to slide a receptacle under her though she knows he will do no such thing.

Intensification of the son's nasty laugh, ha ha ha, piss in your bed then, that'll wash your crotch for you . . .

And with these scurrilous words he takes his cap and bag from the nail and goes off to search for cow-dung.

Pause.

The day begun in this fashion drags on for the sick woman incapable of movement in a silence punctuated by oh la las, time hangs heavy on the hands of this unhappy creature, no clock near her whose hands her eyes could follow to give herself the illusion of progressing towards the twilight in company and thus of having a kind of friend or accomplice in the mechanism, no church clock in the neighborhood either, whose bells would chime out less sad hours which, instead of the dense silence, would add up to a kind of music—crude, certainly, but remotely evoking life, for the hut is in the middle of a forest . . .

Pause.

Who, apart from a few exceptional souls caught up by our only too rare charitable institutions, is capable of imagining the distress of the abandoned bedridden? Whether strangers or others they are legion, whom an outstretched hand could hold back at the edge of the abyss . . .

She is sliding towards it, this loving mother, and will soon sink into it . . .

But night is falling, and her son comes back, yelling.

Longer pause.

And this would be a rough sketch of the density of the second subject, who went off just like that, plunged in his dark thoughts.

And we should not be expected to imagine the destiny of the third one any more than that of the first, for who can say that the second didn't anticipate the third in taking the decision to write, and that hence the lamentable story of the torturer of his mother might equally be that of one of the two others? In the same way the third subject might well have anticipated the second, and that would then prove that strictly speaking none of the three had a destiny, hence the futility of trying to attribute one to anyone by establishing any other fact than this: only the fact of putting pen to paper confers on the hand that has made itself the master of that pen . . . a semblance of reality.

The Chrysanthemum

Man's voice. Tone very much like a confession. Frequent hesitations.

I had to step over a wall or a foundation, let's be quite accurate, a brick or concrete construction, the memory of something rough and cold to the touch, it could be stone, then step over other constructions more or less cold to the touch, now tread on gravel now on grass and stumble into some equally vague foliage . . . Yes but to say tread on, step over, is to exaggerate, given my unstable equilibrium, very weak on my legs, more often flat on the ground than on my feet, crawling as much as walking, falling, standing up again, trial and error . . . A doubt too about what I had come into contact with, my epidermis couldn't be in very good shape, in short all this in the dark, the dense shadows and the scents of the glebe, the earth, the humus, how to put it, to try to forget the word putrefaction . . .

Pause.

For rather than remembering it it's a question of forgetting what for years was responsible for me getting to the point where I could no longer say a word, no longer make a gesture without repenting it, contrition has always been my weakness and was probably my downfall until the day when all activity ceased . . . and I mean all . . . Until the day much much later, it isn't a question of years any more but of God knows what, when in the darkness I once again felt the need to move around, when I couldn't help observing that I was moving around among the constructions in question and that compact darkness, today, that darkness, this new time that I still don't know and that by trial and error I'm going to have to shape, reshape and organize for my own purposes, a poignant thing in itself if it weren't for the still unvanquished fatigue of an ordeal such as no one has ever before undergone, not me at any rate.

Pause.

A note about orientation. On my left, alley number three hundred and thirty-three, a few meters farther on side-alley number seven hundred and seventy-seven crosses it, symbolic numbers if ever there were any but I feel I have a right not to complain about that, let's say not to make any pretensions to a somewhat dubious lucidity.

Pause.

So, to go back to the story of my exit, I had to dodge into alley number three hundred and thirty-three and zigzag along it up to its intersection with the side-alley in order not to lose sight of the numbers written on the metal plates at right angles to each other, and this in spite of the darkness, which comes to the same thing as saying that I stumbled at this spot, that I fell flat on my face, and that the numbers were just a few centimeters away from my nose and I could read them in what may have been a fleeting moonbeam . . . or more plausibly the phosphorescence coming from a nearby tomb . . . unless my eye had become luminous like a cat's, I'll leave the question open.

Pause.

Then my route along side-alley number seven hundred and seventy-seven, no less difficult, no less slow, with its zigzags and occasional obstacles, which were only monuments, swards, piles of dug-up earth, bushes, pots of flowers either botanic, plastic or ceramic . . . which were only the monuments of muck and misery that misfortune accumulates in a feeble head at a turning point as they call it of life, with age and the regression of desire battered by the tempest of the great forgotten myths, evil suddenly regains all its force and leaves you defenseless in the jaws of the ogress, humanity triumphant, the Mother Ubu of nightmare.

Pause.

In that limp, nauseating darkness, it seemed to me that a decision had been taken, but by whom? that I should elect as my domicile an abandoned vault, its chapel grille open and its stone still more or less stable. I leaned against the little greenish altar and I said, this is where I'm going to recover my wits, there was a slate on the ground, maybe left there by a gardener, a slate and a bit of chalk so I could make notes, but what is it like, this new time that I've mentioned, apart from being cut off, fragmentary and furtive, that has this very night come to replace former time like a big, fully-blown flower instead of the expected daisies, and which may be premonitory of eternity, what is it like?

Pause.

Installed in my vault with my slate within reach, it's mild and humid, I only go out at night . . .

Pause.

Wait here for the manifestations of a new life, not despise the little consolations of the former one, you never know, to reject them would be totally out of place since in fact reminiscences are making demands on me.

Pause.

A probable observer, weary of probabilities, perched up in a tree, sees things I cannot discern from my refuge, things are happening outside my range of vision, the slate records them through some phenomenon which is beyond my scope . . . I know too that some sort of action is taking place in the cemetery, controlled, like a ballet or a drama, by an invisible manitou. Characters are moving around. I can hear orders being given. Hear, that's saying a lot, orders, too. Murmurs sensed like vibrations under the skin which coincide with this or that movement of the bodies, or should I say shadowy figures, in this darkness spreading like a patch of oil, the eye gradually becomes

A BIZARRE WILL

accustomed to it, a grey slug crawls along the stone and disappears down a hole, its underground journey . . .

Pause.

Irruption of slugs-hyenas making their way down to the depths of the tombs, at dawn they come back up to the surface, sated and slobbering, then go off to the lettuces in a nearby kitchen garden.

Pause.

It sometimes happens that the observer sees nothing, but the slate goes on recording . . .

Pause.

Description of my refuge. The stone that is freezing my backside, the miniature altar with on the left a cast-iron vase and a little iron candlestick, on the right an antimony crucifix and the mildewy remains of a holy image . . .

Pause.

Tend to conclude that a restricted space, three square meters, is enough for you to be comfortable in, but concede that the wide-open grille may well be a guarantee of a feeling of liberty, it warms your heart to be shivering in front of an opening, a possible escape hole . . .

Pause.

And these slugs after all are the kind that are at home in cellars and underground passages, try not to think of them any more or even to see them as edible creatures, thus eliminating their appearance of necrophagous wild beasts.

Pause.

The slate all the time records the afterlife, eternity, light, entries crossed out and then effaced, but they come back. The relief of no longer being the sole master of one's text. Surprises in vocabulary remain in your head, I dare hope for a renewal of this experience. The absurd amusement of establishing the definitive destination of the present lucubrations . . . Little mandarin games ought to make me laugh now. My simple obsessions will be written somewhere for the benefit of simple souls.

The Chrysanthemum

Pause.

A character in the drama is monologuing indefatigably, I try vainly to listen, he must be with the actors not far from the side-alley in the space where the family tombs form a little island of suffering.

Pause.

The ceiling of the vault was probably made of stones shaped into an arch but it must have disintegrated, it has been roughly replaced by large flat bricks cemented together but not pointed.

A longer pause.

This imposition. Invincible fatigue. The invincible vanquished. Ask oneself in what wretched, nauseating depths the germs of duty survive . . . well, the duty of pursuing the inventory of what is offered to the senses and springs from memory. To call that imagination would be to insult poetry.

Pause.

My exit into the darkness of night. But which night? Certainly not that permanent night whose name may not be pronounced, a remote reference to nocturnal states for the histrion looking for the vague melancholy of the soul, profound, indiscernible darkness of the being and of love. In that case I would have made a theatrical exit. A false exit. I must put up with it. Call on whatever signs may make it acceptable. Even so there is an opening onto something. One can't deceive oneself with impunity, for the imposition was there at the outset. Make punishment the basis of one's only chance of salvation.

Pause.

As for those illocalizable people or rustling sounds, voices from all around, from before, from tonight, from after, a pointless distinction. I am their . . . effacement. Their spokesman . . . Effacement. Write the word again, unaware of what it means for the other people whom my solitude revels in. The former paths reascend up to the same points . . . The difficulty of keeping silent . . . Keeping silent?

Pause.

A BIZARRE WILL

The recollection of special moments when everything seemed possible without the aid of any other presence, but the myth is taking hold again, words no longer suffice to disconcert logic, the mouths that pronounce them find a face again, you fall back into primitive fable-making, this story for incorrigible babes in arms.

Pause.

Put my meeting with Théodore in here.

Pause.

I rather think I made his acquaintance in the following conditions. A cold early morning in October, very bored in my tomb, sleep having deserted me for hours and my rosary between my fingers no longing commanding my attention, all of a sudden a decision has been taken, but again, by whom? the decision to get out. Right away I'm through the grille. I hesitate before starting down the side-alley again. Pains in my knees, legs like jelly . . . I sit down on a nearby sepulcher on which when it gets light I make out, engraved in noble letters, the name of the deceased, Alexandre Mortin. A brief thought for the unknown man. Feeble reflections on the vanity of belle-lettrist inscriptions and the like . . . I was going to take up my rosary again out of indolence when at the intersection, quite a way from the side-alley and from alley number nine hundred and ninety-nine, I think I can see someone. I only have to wait, and not in vain. The character takes shape. It's a young man carrying a pot of chrysanthemums. Unexpected luck, the day of the dead is approaching, this boy has come to put flowers on a grave before the November rush.

Pause.

He had the pale complexion of an aristocrat racked by remorse, a characteristic that isn't so common. My horror of the vulgar was thereby spared, luck had smiled on me. It could have been anyone coming up with chrysanthemums, but this boy corresponded to what in my state I could imagine . . . Effacement.

Pause.

I said to him young man, let's not beat about the bush, sit

The Chrysanthemum

down there and open your heart to me, as you would have to the dead person whose grave you have come to put flowers on, it's so easy in the early morning, and in these circumstances . . . I am full of all the indulgence, pity and softness that could be desired.

Pause.

He plonks it down on the stone in all simplicity, his commemorative flowers too, but remains embarrassed and silent, no doubt so as to seem to want to say a great deal more, a subterfuge that is less rare than his aristocratic appearance.

Pause.

I come out with some vague words about the nip in the air, the matutinal hour, how was it that the cemetery had already opened its gates. He replied that the caretaker had died during the night, which had caused some confusion among the administration, and as he had come very early to wait for the opening he had taken advantage of this momentary disorder. He has not the slightest difficulty in getting up early because sleep has deserted him . . . His eyes mist over. Don't let's be in too much of a hurry . . .

Pause.

He was wearing the latest fashion in trousers, a little American-style denim jacket with patches over the elbows, that's the ultimate in casual elegance with the young people of today, and a hand-knitted, thick woolen scarf.

Pause.

As he didn't open his trap any more I try to get him to confide in me. Have you killed someone? He nods yes. That's nothing, I say, it happens to everyone, nature, ups and downs. Was it by poison, or firearms, or strangulation, or drowning? He was absentmindedly pulling the petals off a chrysanthemum, my question embarrassed him. Well, let's talk about something else then. And turning towards the inscription on the grave, then you knew that Mortin? . . . He jumps, turns around too, stands up, beating heart, and says, he is the person I have come to honor, how comes it . . . what . . .

Pause.

A BIZARRE WILL

He stands there dazed, then gives me a sideways look. Don't worry young man, pull yourself together, nothing unnatural about it, my presence must have distracted you. Then, pointing to my sepulcher, look at my dwelling place instead, a vagabond with no history, no duplicity . . . Tell me about yourself, that will calm you.

I knew Alexandre well, he said, a generous friend, unhappy, persecution complex, failed author, he'd chosen me as his confidant, I learned everything about him.

Pause.

The poor wretch totters, I hold him by the leg, sit down again, which he does and continues his confession, which, the farther it advances the less it holds my attention. In short, held himself responsible, having one day abandoned his benefactor, for the death of the latter a little later.

Pause.

He starts sobbing, I try to console him. Displays of emotion . . . A few entries deleted, then effaced.

Pause.

My name is Théodore, he said, arranging the chrysanthemums as best he could on the marble. And mine is Dieudonné, I said, call me Dodo, if there's anything I can do for you . . .

Pause.

There were forget-me-nots around the edge of the grave, which made me say to the forlorn young man, nothing is sweeter than memories, don't you think? You don't have anyone any more, this is what I suggest. Over there, at the intersection of the side-alley and the alley where you appeared to me, you see that abandoned vault just like mine? Make it your refuge and we'll correspond through our hearts, our thoughts, well, whatever you like . . .

Pause.

And he was already making his way towards the place indicated with a little rawhide suitcase in which he had put his things.

The Chrysanthemum

Pause.

His things, yes . . . That suitcase, when was it that I dared ask him what it contained? One evening no doubt when we were sitting in front of his niche, but as it had just been raining the grass was wet. He pulls out of his suitcase a cloth which he spreads out underneath us. And what else of interest have you in that suitcase, I ask, it isn't curiosity, it's . . . My things, he replies, nothing much, in the way of clothing I have a couple of pairs of socks left and I don't know what else. The important thing is my papers.

Pause.

He shows them to me, arranged in little piles. I ask him are they classified in alphabetical order, chronological order, what are they about? it's fascinating. I was afraid he was going to turn out to be an obsessive collector of God knows what. No though, it was just his things, their order was only apparent. Here, he said, this cutting for example relates part of the speech made at the inauguration of the Suez canal, and this one is the announcement of the engagement of one of my grandmother's uncles, and this photo a little two-month old Newfoundland puppy, and those are my school essays . . .

Pause.

And so on. We were surrounded by the papers. It might have begun to rain again. Let's put them back in the suitcase, I said, we shall get the benefit of them gradually with the passing days, they'll keep us company. And since you seem to be gifted—then I tell him about the slate which had been hidden until then— maybe we could try to write some essays together on the subjects contained in your box of treasures?

Pause.

An absurd idea which would only complicate things by multiplying the number of the irresponsible.

Pause.

He put away his cuttings, they were held together by bits of string, rubber bands, clothes pins. Paid no attention to me for a long moment. Then put his suitcase back in the left-hand corner of his niche saying forget what's worrying you Monsieur Dodo, it can't be really serious. Looking at you one envies your diaphanous state. Everything can be seen on your face. It won't do you any good to cross out, delete, efface . . . Consider me a little like your slate, I will only remember what you want me to of your words . . .

Pause.

I had thought I saw innocence in his eyes. Was it perfidy?

Pause.

Traces of effacement.

A longer pause.

All the June flowers, cornflower, poppy, pheasant's eye, betony, cow-wheat, love-in-a-mist, white campion, centaury, hempnettle, coronilla, bugle, St. John's wort, Venus's navelwort, sweet clover, hemlock, honeysuckle, speedwell, broom, water iris, yellow rattle, self-heal, meadow sage, butter-and-eggs, marjoram, delphinium . . .

Pause.

A fearful avalanche.

Pause. The voice becomes more hesitant.

Who will take account of this passionate innocence . . . the innocence that causes the resurgence of the old myths, cockchafers of despair?

Pause.

The lilies of the big sleep . . .

Pause.

Oasis of the night . . .

Pause.

The meeting in the cemetery . . . That suitcase full of treasures . . .

Pause. Guffaws. Pause.

Alone . . .

The Chrysanthemum

> *Pause.*

The slate in smithereens . . .

> *A longer pause. The speaker's tone suddenly becomes affirmative, but without grandiloquence.*

All regrets stifled. Task accepted.

> *Pause.*

To recompose as a defense against anguish, no matter where it may come from, that unforgotten dream . . . then finally leave it far behind, an old ceiling cluttered with birds and flowers in the taste of a bygone age, and progress toward the inaccessible . . . without landmarks, without erasures, without notes of any kind, unattainable but present . . . which must be believed in for fear of never dying.

Crazy Notion

A, B, *men's voices.*

A. What did you say?
B. Me? Nothing.
A. You said something.
B. Don't remember.

A few seconds' silence.

A. You won't dispute it this time?
B. What?
A. You know.
B. I tell you I don't.
A. I tell you you do. (*Pause.*) Funny way to deny the obvious. You won't get me to believe it's just modesty. Fear of what? Of me? Don't make me laugh.
B. Laugh your head off. Your attitude exasperates me.
A. As if it was mine! (*Pause.*) Whatever you do, you won't get away from it.
B. Get away from what?
A. You can answer that yourself.

A BIZARRE WILL

B. The urge to follow that absurd line? I lost it a long time ago.
A. You're gradually getting into it in spite of yourself, and your shame is superfluous, at your age.
B. What's my age got to do with it?
A. Everything.
B. Because in your opinion . . .
A. In my opinion! You're making me very important all of a sudden.

A few seconds' silence.

A. Well?
B. I . . .
A. You . . . ?
B. It's a dog's life. Nauseating. Makes you want to do yourself in. All this sordid old . . .
A. People oughtn't to be too hard on themselves. There's still a lot to be got out of it. We're powerless against the demands of memory.
B. Its demands?
A. What it repeats, and will go on repeating until the end.
B. That broken voice, that drivel . . . A fine monument to the glory of humanity.
A. Humanity! You aren't going to claim . . .
B. No, not really.

A few seconds' silence.

A. Well then?
B. There's an army on the march . . . dust swirling up . . . groans . . . then suddenly a stifled cry . . . stifled cries . . . (*Pause.*) Is it an army on the march? No, it's the scenery going by . . . People used to talk about the beauty of ruins . . . A nightmare, yes . . . I'm not up to it any more . . .
A. You *must* be. (*Pause.*) An aqueduct? A temple? An amphitheater? (*A little laugh.*) A stone, isn't it? With inscriptions . . . A for acquisition, B for blessing, C for capture, D for demand . . .
B. For desertion.
A. E for error . . .
B. No order in all that, it'd be too easy . . . (*Pause.*) They stopped by the stone, they tried to read it, for a long time, taking it in turns, passing the word on to each other . . . I

can't hear very well . . . The word past or the word last . . . For a long time. Men of good will. (*Little laugh.*) Finally they all fell asleep there, in a heap, exhausted . . . (*Pause.*) A vulture so soon . . . Sky permanently blue . . . A huge sun? No, diffused light . . .

A. Something must have happened.
B. Before?
A. Yes. Everything that gets organized around . . . a hearth . . . (*Pause.*) It's a hearth, that stone, it can't be anything else. And the inscriptions—are prescriptions. Pathetic mysteries transmitted from one generation to the next, and so deformed that the disease is taken for the cure and vice versa . . . Something like that, don't you think?
B. Maybe. It'd be better to listen to the people who are sleeping . . . or dying . . . Difficult, difficult . . .

A few seconds' silence.

B. They're the ones talking about the army on the march, the dust, the hearth . . . I didn't see anything . . . All in the same voice . . . (*He whispers.*): Absence of voice . . . Whispers . . .
A. Listen . . . listen harder . . . go closer . . . They said we should strain our ears . . . There are subtle differences in those whispers, they don't all articulate in the same way . . .
B. Subtle differences . . . maybe . . . so faint . . . minimal . . . (*Pause.*) I can hear the word "beginning" . . . and "restarting" . . . and "redoing" . . . and "reopening" . . . yes, reopening . . . what?
A. Their eyes?
B. I think their eyes are already open . . . (*Pause.*) They're talking about the scenery . . . the desert . . . about trees somewhere else, meadows somewhere else . . . about water . . . They're thirsty . . . (*Pause.*) No. They're recumbent figures . . . they can only see the sky . . . An army of recumbent figures with their eyes open and their hands clasped together, around that stone which brings them to the attention of . . . to the attention . . .
A. Maybe of another army on the march coming to their rescue?
B. Unlikely. (*Pause.*) Who was talking of a vulture? Imagination . . .
A. No, memory.

A BIZARRE WILL

B. Or that they said vulture instead of imagination?

A few seconds' silence.

A. I can see them. They're in star-formation around the stone. They're made of marble, and the stone is granite. Perfect alignment, perfect symmetry. There's something to be got out of that. No hurry . . . plenty of time . . . We shall find out, we have to find out . . . The center and what radiates from it. (*Pause.*) Their hands aren't clasped together . . . They're stretching their arms out sideways, all holding each other's hands . . . a slight swaying movement . . . an undulation like a wave . . . the circles made by a stone thrown into the water which spread outward and disappear into the distance . . . We're on the open sea.

B. The ocean of vicissitudes . . . (*Little laugh.*)

A. Can't you hear the sound of the waves?

Pause.

B. Yes. And the wind that drowns the cry . . . No one knows where it came from . . .

A. There are other centers and other things being radiated . . . (*Pause.*) No, it isn't the sea . . . A mosaic seen from very high up . . .

B. The eye of the vulture.

A. It's there, yes . . . watching . . . and waiting . . .

A few seconds' silence.

B. What else?

A. I can't see anything else. We've wandered . . . (*Pause.*) Not paying attention.

B. Wanting to put everything into words . . .

A. Not paying attention. Off the track . . .

B. Let's forget about this crazy notion.

A. No. We have to find out. (*Pause.*) Listen harder. (*Pause.*) Still those whispers?

B. I may have been wrong about their number . . . Maybe only one person's whispers . . . A single head, everything in it is all mixed up . . . (*Pause.*) That army or that cohort . . . No—too simple. A single head . . . for everybody's anguish?

From very far off comes the sound of a man's cry, echoed two or three times. It stops abruptly.

Crazy Notion

A. Possible. (*Pause.*) I can't see it yet . . .
B. A single throat for everybody's cry . . . Corny. (*Little laugh.*)
A. Listen.
B. Why insist?

Another cry, ditto.

A. This time I can see him. He's standing in front of the stone, he's deciphering the inscription. (*Pause.*) He's very familiar . . . that long face, that bent back, the pilgrim's staff, the haversack over his shoulder . . . It's all there. (*Pause.*) Incapable of crying out. He isn't the one who's crying out.
B. Another scapegoat?
A. No. There was no cry. Only a squall. A storm, the raging sea . . . (*Pause.*) Can you still hear it?
B. No.
A. The old man's moving away from the stone. He's given up trying to decipher it. He's leaving . . . We've often seen him going off, back to the grey hills . . . It was waves, quite simply . . . He's going back there to set sail again . . . He'll never be shipwrecked . . .
B. What's the good of tormenting ourselves? This kind of discovery . . . Symbol, allegory, hodgepodge . . .
A. Could there be anything better to do? What else? (*Pause.*) Dig deep, come up with the solution . . . That nomad—we have to find out what he's looking for. And why he's deceiving us under other . . . many other . . . evanescent appearances . . . (*Pause.*) We have to understand, that's to say weigh things up. It's the imponderable that does the damage. (*Pause.*) Are you listening?
B. Yes. The imponderable. Something that can't be weighed, so it will always do damage.
A. Well then, the things that can't be weighed—we'll have to deal with them. Arrive at some lucid ideas. (*Pause.*) What's the meaning of that army, those recumbent figures, that center and its rays? Images of humanity on the march or in waiting? Humanity! An old abyss of laziness that can be dramatized by not paying attention? Cheap moral? (*Pause.*) And the pilgrim? Another old clown among the hodgepodge of the inheritance? He imposed on us long enough . . . deluged us with his jeremiads . . . Deceived us under other,

many other appearances, a Proteus of the derisory . . . (*Pause.*) Are you listening?

> *Sound of the wind for a few seconds. It stops abruptly.*

A. Are you listening?

> *Sound of the wind, ditto. A few seconds' silence.*

A. You weren't there. (*Pause.*) Hackneyed myths . . . You're one of them, too . . . I'd thought I'd be able to . . . Crazy notion, you said . . . You? A figure of speech. (*Pause.*) I heard something . . . Heard? (*Pause.*) Neither the wind, nor the sea, nor even a voice . . . (*Pause.*) To be alone? To have said I am alone? Me? Didn't open my mouth. (*Pause.*) Didn't see anything, either, I'm blind, you remember . . . (*Pause.*) That army on the march, that sea, that mosaic . . . (*Pause.*) Literature? (*A little laugh. Pause.*) The vulture, perhaps . . . (*Pause.*) They said vulture instead of imagination . . . Perched on the top of that mountain peak, you remember, it's watching, it's waiting . . . Dangerous? No! A poor, hungry animal. (*Pause.*) It must have seen me lying here near this stone and taken me for its prey . . . It's watching, it's waiting . . . (*Pause.*) My arms are outstretched, am I moving? No. Paralyzed. Fear? Of what? Of the vulture? I can't see it. (*Pause.*) Lying here near this stone, paralyzed . . . (*Pause.*) Dying? Am I dying? No, you don't die without knowing it. Nonsense. (*Pause.*) A ready-made prey for the carrion-eater . . . Sky permanently blue . . . A huge sun? Diffused light? The blind man cannot answer. (*Pause.*) His arms are outstretched, he . . . (*Pause.*) Dying? Is he dying?

> *The cry of the vulture is heard, quite near. Then, very soon after, a loud sound of wings, very close to the mike, followed by the death rattle of a man being choked.*

Night

Voices of AL, BEN
then of A, B and ANNOUNCER

This play was first broadcast by Radio Stuttgart in 1972, in the translation by Gerda Scheffel.

    Both actors speak very close to the microphone.

AL. What's that I hear?
BEN. What's that you hear?
AL. Listen.

    Sound of a cricket chirping. Ten seconds. It stops the moment one of the characters speaks.

  It's a cricket.
BEN. In February? You're joking.
AL. I tell you it's a cricket. Listen.

    Chirping of cricket. Five seconds.

BEN. You're round the bend. Or else you've got wax or I don't know what in your ears.
AL. It stops when we speak. Shh, listen.

Chirping of cricket. Five seconds.

A cricket in our room! Like bakers had in the old days. They bring good luck.
BEN. I tell you you're off your trolley, Al. There's no more a cricket here than there is a . . .
AL. Some people don't hear them. I remember my grandmother . . .
BEN. Leave your grandmother in peace and go to sleep. I'm tired.

Chirping of cricket. Ten seconds.

AL. Ben.
BEN. Mm?
AL. It'd be wonderful to buy that house.
BEN. Where'd we get the cash? We haven't got more than a quarter of what we'd need.
AL. Couldn't we beat her down? Or pay by instalments? It'd take a bit of time, that's all.
BEN. She wants cash.
AL. The old skinflint.
BEN. Leave the old woman in peace and go to sleep, I'm tired.

Chirping of cricket. Five seconds.

AL. You're always tired. I'm not sleepy.
BEN. Count your crickets, then.
AL. There's only one, I think. Shh . . .

Chirping of cricket. Five seconds.

Yes, just one.
BEN. Well, imagine a whole bunch of crickets in a meadow and count them.
AL. They never get together. They're solitary insects. Not like grasshoppers. Do you remember the grasshoppers at Fantoine?
BEN. They were locusts.
AL. They don't make the same sound as crickets. It's harsher. I'm sure the old woman's meadow is full of locusts in the

Night

summer. In the lucerne and the sainfoin. Oh Ben, it'd be wonderful. Couldn't we borrow some money?
BEN. Who from? Our pals are all broke.
AL. There's banks that lend money, there's special places . . .
BEN. You need to be what they call creditworthy, have a fixed wage, guarantees. We don't have anything.
AL. Maybe I could work in an office?
BEN. I can just see you in an office! You wouldn't last three days.
AL. What do you know about it?
BEN. What do I know about it? You can't go an hour without sketching something or other. All you can do is draw, and not just any sort of drawing, at that, but your own sort, your thingummies.
AL. Is that bad?
BEN. It's very good. And now let me go to sleep.

Chirping of cricket. Ten seconds.

AL. Ben.
BEN. Mm?
AL. I'm a bit fed up with this place. Don't you think we ought to make a change? In the country it'd be another life. Aren't *you* fed up with this room and that courtyard and the concierge who never stops bellyaching?
BEN. More than fed up.
AL. You ought to write thrillers. They'd sell like hot cakes.
BEN. I've tried. I'm no good at it. The only thing I can do is dialogue. Without the occasional radio commission I'd have been on my uppers long ago.
AL. Well then . . . a love story? A sentimental thing . . .
BEN. Sentiment . . . for all the good *that's* done me . . .
AL. Don't you love me any more?
BEN. Yes, Al, but it isn't . . .
AL. It isn't what? Exciting?
BEN. If you like. But I'm not complaining. That's life.
AL. That's life.

Chirping of cricket. Ten seconds.

Ben.
BEN. Mm?
AL. I don't feel so good.
BEN. What's the matter?

AL. It hurts a bit here.
BEN. Where?
AL. Here.
BEN. Your stomach?
AL. No, higher up.
BEN. What's it feel like?
AL. I don't know. Like a sort of cramp.
BEN. Would you like a sedative?
AL. Do you have one?
BEN. An aspirin.
AL. I don't know. It'll pass.

Chirping of cricket. Ten seconds.

BEN. Feeling better?
AL. Yes. I'm thinking about that house.
BEN. Well, go on thinking about it and try to sleep.
AL. Yes—but it keeps me awake. Do you remember how many windows there are? Two on the ground floor in the front wall, plus the glass door, and two above. And on the other side, two or three? Then there's that little skylight, I don't remember what shape it is. Why doesn't the old woman sell in return for a life annuity? That'd be the best solution, don't you think?
BEN. Mmm.
AL. Are you asleep?
BEN. Mmm.
AL. That'd be a great saving. How much per month could she ask? They don't spend anything at that age.

Chirping of cricket, combined with a regular, muffled beating sound: heartbeats. Ten seconds.

Living room downstairs with a big fireplace and leather armchairs and sheepskin rugs. And a bar with plenty of bottles and a record player and a TV tucked away in an old cupboard. Nothing but old stuff that we'd go and haggle over with the junk dealers like when we furnished that millionairess's house, what was her name, it was in the Loire or the Indre-et-Loire or the Loir-et-Cher . . .

*On its own, the regular, muffled beating sound.
Ten seconds.*

Night

Al lowers his voice slightly.

And the kitchen with modern gadgets, aluminum sink, and hotplates, and fridge, or rather no, we'd cook in the big fireplace, nothing but old-fashioned utensils, frying pans, kettles, stewpans, grills, spits, and the lavatory in the little room, or rather no, at the top of the stairs with a really modern bathroom, yellow and blue tiles, yes, with . . . with . . .

Slightly louder beating sound. Ten seconds.

Ben.

Pause.

Ben.

Slightly louder beating sound. Five seconds.

Voice even lower.

Downstairs the living room with a big fireplace and leather chairs and sheepskin rugs cook in the fireplace grills kettles grills preserving pans kettles why doesn't she sell in return for a life annuity that'd be a great saving you haven't got much longer that'd bring you in so much per month ask my friend he has a head for business he's really someone . . .

Slightly louder beating sound. Five seconds.

Ben.

Pause.

Ben!

BEN (*waking up with a start*): What? What is it? What's the matter?

AL. I don't feel so good. Give me that aspirin.

Sound of light switch, then of drawer being opened, faint rustles, and water being poured into a glass.

BEN. Here. Sit up.
AL. Thanks. Pull the pillow up.

Pause.

D'you mind if we leave the light on for a bit?
BEN. No. I'm not sleepy any more.

A BIZARRE WILL

AL. Can you guess what I'd like?
BEN. What?
AL. You to read me a few pages of Don Quixote.
BEN. Monsieur wants to act the spoilt child? If you like.

Pause.
Sound of pages being turned over.

What d' you want me to read?
AL. The end.
BEN (*reading*): "As all human things, especially the lives of men, are transitory, being ever on the decline from their beginnings till they reach their final end, and as Don Quixote had no privilege from Heaven exempting him from the common fate, his dissolution and end came when he least expected it. Whether that event was brought on by melancholy occasioned by the contemplation of his defeat or whether it was by divine ordination, a fever seized him and kept him to his bed for six days, during which time he was frequently visited by his friends, the priest, the Bachelor and the barber, and his good squire Sancho Panza never left his bedside.

"All of them believed that grief at his overthrow and the disappointment of his hopes for Dulcinea's deliverance and disenchantment had brought him to this state, and tried to cheer him in every possible way. The Bachelor bade him be of good heart, and get up and begin on his pastoral life, for which he had already composed an eclogue, which would knock out every one Sannazaro had ever written. He said that he had bought a couple of fine dogs with his own money from a herdsman from Quitanar to guard the flock, one called Barcino and the other Butron. But Don Quixote's dejection persisted all the same. His friends called in a doctor, who took his pulse and did not offer much comfort, saying that he should certainly attend to the salvation of his soul, for his body's was in danger. Don Quixote heard this with a quiet mind, but not so his housekeeper, his niece and his squire, who began to weep piteously, as if he already lay dead before their eyes. It was the doctor's opinion that melancholy and despondency were bringing him to his end. Don Quixote begged to be left alone, for he wanted to sleep a little. They obeyed him, and he slept for more than six hours, at a stretch as they say; so long, in fact, that his

Night

housekeeper and his niece thought that he would pass away in his sleep. But at the end of that time he woke and cried out loudly: 'Blessed be Almighty God, who has vouchsafed me this great blessing! Indeed his mercies are boundless, nor can the sins of men limit or hinder them.'"

AL. Is this where he makes his will in favor of Sancho?
BEN. Two pages further on.

Sound of pages being turned.

"The clerk went in with the others and, after he had drawn up the heads of the will, Don Quixote disposed of his soul with all the requisite Christian formalities and came to the bequests saying:

"'*Item, this is my will regarding certain moneys which Sancho Panza, whom in my madness I made my squire, retains, there having been between him and me certain accounts, receipts and disbursements. I wish him not to be charged with them, nor asked to account for them, but if there should be any surplus after he has paid himself what I owe him, the residue is to be his. It will be very little, and may it do him much good. And if when I was mad I was party to giving him the governorship of an isle, now that I am sane I would give him a kingdom, were I able, for the simplicity of his nature and the fidelity of his conduct deserve it.*'

"Then, turning to Sancho, he said: 'Pardon me, friend, that I caused you to appear mad, like me, making you fall into the same sort of error as myself, the belief that there were and still are knights errant in the world.'

"'Oh, don't die, dear master!' answered Sancho in tears. 'Take my advice and live many years. For the maddest thing a man can do in this life is to let himself die just like that, without anybody killing him, but just finished off by his own melancholy. Don't be lazy, look you, but get out of bed, and let's go out into the fields dressed as shepherds, as we decided to. Perhaps we shall find the lady Dulcinea behind some hedge, disenchanted and as pretty as a picture. If it's from grief at being beaten you're dying, put the blame on me and say you were tumbled off because I girthed Rocinante badly. For your worship must have seen in your books of chivalries that it's a common thing for one knight to overthrow another, and the one that's conquered today may be the conqueror tomorrow.'

A BIZARRE WILL

"At last Don Quixote's end came, after he had received all the sacraments and expressed his horror of books of chivalry in strong and moving terms. The clerk, who happened to be present, said that he had never read in any book of chivalries of a knight errant dying in his bed in so calm and Christian a manner as Don Quixote."

> *Pause. Then the muffled beating sound returns. Five seconds.*

AL. Why is that story just as beautiful, wherever, whenever and however you read it?
BEN. A lot of art, they say, in the writing; a lot of science.
AL. Couldn't we say a lot of poetry, and all the love in the world?
BEN. We could say that, yes.

> *Pause.*

Don't you want me to finish it? There's still the last page.
AL (*voice still lower*): I think I'll go to sleep.

> *Pause. Sound of the light switch. Then the muffled beating sound again, becoming fainter. Fifteen seconds. It stops. Pause.*

BEN (*in an undertone*): Are you asleep?

> *Pause.*

Are you asleep?

> *Pause.*

Al, are you asleep?

> *Pause. He suddenly shouts:*

Al! Are you asleep? Al! Al! Al. . . .

> *Sound of a radio being switched off.*

A *and* B, *two different voices. Tone of an ordinary conversation.*

A. So that's the famous commission?

Night

B. What do you think of it?

Pause.

I had to make Al die. Didn't it work?
A. Not work?—I wouldn't say it didn't work. Let's say it's a bit high-flown. And just after the death of Don Quixote, really . . .
B. I *had* to quote that text, that everyone's forgotten.
A. It should have been one or the other. Either Don Quixote or Al who meets his end. But not both.
B. I also needed the parallel between two friendships, two understandings. Does that bother you?
A. I needed, I needed . . . I won't say it bothers me, but if you want my opinion . . .
B. I do.
A. I repeat: it shouldn't be overdone.
B. It's theater.
A. Theater or radio?
B. What's the difference?
A. Monsieur wants some theory? Radio—closer, transposition less apparent.
B. Naturalism?
A. Nothing to do with it. But nuances, nuances . . . Basically, though, you aren't interested in my opinion.
B. Actually, I'd have liked there to be *more* nuances.
A. As for instance?
B. As for instance, if you'd said the quotation was too long, or Ben's shout too loud, or the chirping of the cricket inexplicable . . .
A. As a matter of fact, yes. How do you justify the cricket?
B. It makes the listener identify instantly with Al's fever. The chirping sound is what the sick man hears. Just as the heart beating is his own. A subjective mike.
A. People don't necessarily understand.
B. They *should* understand. It depends on the actors.
A. Even so, the best thing in your story is when Don Quixote says about Sancho: "Were I able, now that I am sane I would give him a kingdom . . ."
B. And when Sancho says to Don Quixote: "Oh, don't die, dear master, but take my advice, for the maddest thing a man can do in this life is to let himself die just like that . . ."

A BIZARRE WILL

Pause.

A. Well?
B. Well nothing. Everything has been said—a long time before us.
A. Would that be any reason not to write any more?
B. My goodness . . .

A gong is sounded lightly. Then, the voice of the usual announcer of this series of plays:

ANNOUNCER: You have been listening to "Night," a divertissement for radio by Robert Pinget. As the author is a perfectionist, he would be grateful if listeners would kindly let him know their opinion of this sketch. Please write to . . .

About Nothing

Two men's voices

A. About nothing.
B. How d'you mean, about nothing?
A. To talk. To talk about nothing.
B. What? Just like that?
A. Just like that.
B. You phone, it's urgent, you arrive, you're here . . . and nothing?
A. Write first—I did think about it. Thought hard. Didn't know. So phoned.
B. Urgent.
A. But even the phone . . .
B. What about the phone?
A. Better than writing, but it goes too fast, you tie yourself up in knots, you lose the thread . . .
B. You mix your metaphors.
A. Very funny. You know what I mean.
B. No, believe it or not.
A. Well try then. I'm hesitating—shall I write? I phone. That's no good. What've I got left.

B. What've you got left?
A. To see you. To see you—that's all.
B. Well, here I am.
A. Me too.
B. Right. But we still have to . . .
A. You always want reasons.
B. Excuse me, but it was you . . .
A. You want reasons. To know why, to conclude, always to conclude.
B. In this case I don't see how.
A. I'm not asking *that* much of you.
B. But what little you *are* asking . . . ?
A. Nothing, once again.
B. Yes you are. To listen to you. Something to confide to me, to communicate, something that bothers you. Be simple—just tell me.
A. Simple. Communicate . . . Words, talk, chat.
B. Ye-es. Well, let's not say anything. Even so, I'm listening.
A. You'll never change.
B. Don't tell me you'd rather I did.
A. I'm not saying that.
B. But?
A. Nothing.
B. Yes you are. You resent my . . . What d'you expect, age . . .
A. Not a question of age.
B. Of what, then?
A. Don't know. I'll leave you.
B. No, don't go. Here, have a drink.
A. Is this a new wine?
B. Yes. Not bad?
A. Good, even. I'd have liked . . . No that's idiotic. I'd have liked . . . Interaction.
B. What?
A. Dream and reality. Interaction. I'd have liked . . .
B. Spit it out. Liked what?
A. Not a question of age. Some people are old at twenty. In the old days, you'd . . .
B. I'd have understood you, but not any more, right, go on.
A. Very good, your plonk . . . The things you dream of or envisage or even begin to achieve . . .
B. I see. Your work?

About Nothing

A. If it *is* work, yes.
B. Started what? You were doing a dialogue. And it got sidetracked?
A. I don't know if that's the right word. But the dialogue's had it.
B. A dialogue about having nothing to say, maybe? Answer me. About having nothing to say?
A. Something of the sort.
B. Oh well. Go on. The dialogue's had it. There's still monologue, though.
A. But what *is* monologue?
B. When you talk to yourself.
A. Out of the question. Always an ear there.
B. Right. Go on.
A. Some lucky people have a message to communicate.
B. Not true. Nothing to say—that's the gift.
A. Aha! Trapped!
B. Excuse me—your mind isn't on your work. There are *two* of us, and we're trying . . .
A. But what if my work was aimed at forgetting it?
B. Don't understand.
A. Oh well. Work or not, we're talking for the sake of talking. Saying nothing at great length. That's important. For me at the moment at any rate.
B. That reminds me of something I heard—authentic. A chap mumbling to his pal: I'm not chatting to you for the sake of talking, but just to tell you.
A. Quite nice. But me, it's neither to tell you nor to talk that I'm here, it's to chat.
B. Your turn to be trapped. You said it was to see me. What was all that about dream and reality?
A. Nothing more than this—the point we've reached. I'm dreaming . . . about your reality . . . or about mine . . . How can I put it?
B. Finish your wine.
A. In vino veritas? Not true. Wine has only ever revealed surface worries, passing irritations. Which goes to show that the old proverbs . . .
B. Torments, anxieties, which surface after a drink or two.
A. No, I tell you. When we're drunk there's no question of revealing anything of our inner depths.

A BIZARRE WILL

B. Do they exist?
A. I think so. Or let's say anything serious, weighty, important. Which you need a lot of lucidity to formulate.
B. And which you were trying to formulate in your work that didn't come off?
A. I think so, yes.
B. Bet you anything you like it had to do with your life, with talking about it in the most authentic possible tone, no? Come on—just a little effort.
A. Which doesn't stop one getting the tone wrong. But you're probably right. My life. A word I detest.
B. Existence, then?
A. Worse.
B. Happiness?
A. Let's not talk drivel.
B. It's not drivelling to hope for it. The only possible way. Although obviously . . .
A. Obviously what?
B. Everyone wants a different sort.
A. Thank God.
B. Are you implying that mine, the happiness *I* want, is very different from yours?
A. I didn't say that. But other people's, everyone else's, *is*.
B. What do we care?
A. A lot. Responsible. We're responsible for it. That's all that matters.
B. For other people's happiness?
A. Of course.
B. Then why say Thank God?
A. The difficulty. If there's nothing to overcome, there's no solution.
B. Your mania for moralizing.
A. My life or not, it's more or less that . . . that's what I wanted to free myself from . . . more or less that, yes.
B. A splendid programme. But you don't feel up to it.
A. No.
B. Selfishness, well yes. It's the same for everyone. It was quite simple, your need to confide in someone.
A. Simple? The last thing anyone can bring himself to admit.
B. To me? You're joking.

About Nothing

A. I mean to recognize. A hell of a job to get rid of it. Unless selfishness and self-love are two different things?
B. Do you doubt it? Seems to me as simple as ABC. But I'm just quoting the catechism. Sorry.
A. Your reality. You there in front of me—I'm dreaming you, I'm imagining you the way you used to be but aren't any more.
B. It's age, I tell you—that's simple. But you—not the same?
A. Yes. But you irritate me with your "simplicity." What's the catechism got to do with it?
B. Just a manner of speaking . . . of saying nothing.
A. Of saying nothing serious. You're wriggling out of it.
B. Need to know what you're getting at.
A. I was saying selfishness and self-love.
B. You say a lot of things whether you're talking or not, I can't make head or tail of them. Love thy neighbor as thyself, that comes in the catechism, doesn't it?
A. And selfishness—what is *that*?
B. Forgetting your neighbor.
A. Then there are two sorts of love, one good and one bad. How can we distinguish between them? Where does self-love stop and love for other people begin?
B. That's just it, it's a trap. A huge joke. Balance impossible to achieve.
A. You're avoiding my question.
B. You see, you *are* questioning me. You've come to have a discussion and not to say nothing.
A. Just a manner of speaking. One worries, one wonders . . .
B. *You* worry, *you* torment yourself. I was right. You really please me. However much you dream me, I remain the same. And you too. In other words . . .
A. In other words?
B. Not possible for anyone to open his trap for nothing. Just one word and it all comes tumbling out, the whole shebang. Yes, you really please me.
A. Selfishness. Problem not solved.
B. Don't you think that's simpler? It's solving it that's difficult. Another glass?
A. Your lousy plonk.
B. Shall we go on? Still saying nothing, of course.
A. I've been thinking all day about what I was saying yesterday or just now . . . Dialogue or monologue full of great ideas,

not my own. A few authors that I still read. No question of naming them.
B. Moralists, philosophers, historians . . .
A. Nor even of quoting them, for fear of betraying them.
B. Do what with them then?
A. Orient our thought towards theirs. Slightly. Got off on the wrong foot. Desultory. Desultory conversation from which it would emerge that . . . that what's big is very small.
B. Eh?
A. A face, for example.
B. A face?
A. A beautiful face. Describe it. Nobility, purity, in short, go in for abstraction, whereas its beauty lies in its gaze. And in that gaze there's something minute to which you simply can't give a name.
B. The window of the soul.
A. If you talk about the soul every other minute you'll have betrayed something that only exists through its secrecy.
B. What're you supposed to do, then? Go all bug-eyed?
A. No. But not indulge in fine words. There's only one that matters; say it at all costs. The greater the difficulty, the more exalted will be . . . what ought to be exalted.
B. The soul, then.
A. That's a cop-out.
B. Are you backing down?
A. A serious question is answered by a paradox. The most honest. And I'm thinking again about the gift, the talent, that makes people admire the person who possesses it. Now the artist, the real artist, doesn't recognize himself in it, the gift is foreign to him, it's come from somewhere else. Hostile, even—an enemy. A life and death struggle between them.
B. Don't understand.
A. Poetry, painting, music. Something enormous, admirable in other people. But yourself, if you're gifted, it's hard for you to see it as enormous. It's very small, and most of the time it isn't there. The gift only asserts itself when it's taken for a defect, a lack.
B. How does the artist become aware of it, then?
A. The "how" can't be explained. Stronger than any reasoning. The gift can only be recognized in the work.
B. In other words, anyone . . .

About Nothing

A. Not true. To claim that everyone is a poet is stupid.
B. Your paradoxes get on my nerves. We started off intending to say nothing.
A. What have we said?
B. I—nothing. But you . . .
A. I? You want to know something? I can take back everything I've just come out with and maintain the opposite, in all honesty. Everyone is gifted in his own way, no one is responsible for other people's happiness, selfishness and self-love are one and the same, fine thoughts are not the prerogative of any privileged person, what is big cannot by definition be small, the soul . . . What was it we said about the soul?
B. I—nothing.
A. I formulated something or other.
B. Only exists through its secrecy.
A. Only exists through the absence of all secrecy.
B. That doesn't mean anything.
A. Precisely. You see—we've come back to our point of departure.
B. Another glass?
A. The last.
B. Shall we go on?
A. Some other time.